Ghost Towns of
Ontario's Cottage Country

GHOST TOWNS

OF

ONTARIO'S COTTAGE COUNTRY

ANDREW HIND

DUNDURN
PRESS

Publisher: Kwame Scott Fraser | Acquiring editor: Kathryn Lane | Editor: Michael Carroll
Cover designer: Karen Alexiou
Cover image: top to bottom: Courtesy Mary Fitzmaurice, Gloria Cassidy, Bracebridge Public Library, Brian Dobbs; background: Eva Bronzini / pexels.com
Interior part opener image: Archives of Ontario, I0050469

Library and Archives Canada Cataloguing in Publication

Title: Ghost towns of Ontario's cottage country / Andrew Hind.
Names: Hind, Andrew, author.
Description: Includes bibliographical references and index.
Identifiers: Canadiana (print) 20220484309 | Canadiana (ebook) 20220484333 | ISBN 9781459751132 (softcover) | ISBN 9781459751149 (PDF) | ISBN 9781459751156 (EPUB)
Subjects: LCSH: Ghost towns—Ontario. | LCSH: Ghost towns—Ontario—Guidebooks. | LCSH: Ontario—History, Local. | LCSH: Ontario—Description and travel. | LCSH: Ontario—Guidebooks.
Classification: LCC FC3070.G4 H56 2023 | DDC 971.3—dc23

We acknowledge the support of the Canada Council for the Arts and the Ontario Arts Council for our publishing program. We also acknowledge the financial support of the Government of Ontario, through the Ontario Book Publishing Tax Credit and Ontario Creates, and the Government of Canada.

Dundurn Press
1382 Queen Street East
Toronto, Ontario, Canada M4L 1C9
dundurn.com, @dundurnpress ▶ f ◎

To Nicoletta, my wife, my friend, and the mother of our daughter. You inspire me. This book is dedicated to you.

CONTENTS

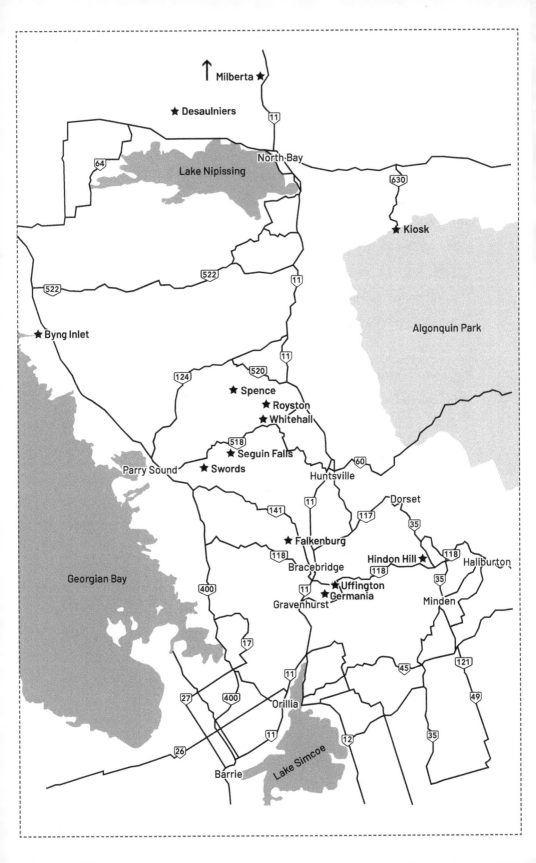

INTRODUCTION

A building leans wearily with age, lurking behind a veil of green foliage. Worn stairs, their wood splintering, lead up to a rotting porch. Thick spiderwebs hang like drapes from under the porch and along the building's eaves. Windows are shaded filth. A ghostly aura hangs heavily in the air.

That was my introduction to Ontario's ghost towns some 40 years ago. I've been intrigued by them ever since. In childhood, my mind conjured up lurid stories associated with these forsaken buildings. As an adult, in my career as historian and writer, I came to appreciate that I didn't need to create fantastical tales. The real stories of vanished villages these buildings survived were every bit as dramatic as anything I could imagine. I made it a mission to research such ghost towns and bring them back from the dead, if only on the printed page.

It's a big job. Ontario has hundreds of ghost towns — communities that lived, sometimes only briefly, but have faded with the passage of time. This book concerns itself with 13 ghost towns from across the region loosely defined as cottage country: Muskoka and Parry Sound Districts, Haliburton County, Algonquin Park, and the near north above Lake Nipissing.

As late as the middle of the 19th century, this area remained a remote, unsettled wilderness to colonial surveyors, barely charted, foreboding in its darkness and silence. Only a few European explorers and fur traders had passed through the territory, let alone mapped it. For colonizers, it was almost a complete blank space on maps. To them, the region's impenetrable forests, ever-present rock, and countless swamps would have seemed imposing and intimidating.

Although alien and distant to settlers and surveyors from the south, the region was well known to the Anishinaabeg, who have lived there for thousands of years, hunting, trapping, and using the interconnected rivers and lakes as seasonal highways. Today, there are a number of Anishinaabeg land claims in cottage country and Northern Ontario, in particular one by the Nipissing (Nbisiing) First Nation, stemming from the Robinson Huron Treaty made with the British in 1850, which the Nipissing argue hasn't been properly honoured and needs renewal.

It was only in the middle of the 19th century that the colonial government of Upper Canada, now called Canada West, began contemplating settling this vast region. By then, all the farmland had been taken up in Southern Ontario and settlers were demanding the government open more land and more districts. A flood of European immigrants — 100,000 Irish arrived in 1847 alone — added urgency to these calls.

At the same time, lumber interests began to pressure the colonial government to open the area for settlement. They knew that settlers meant roads, a ready pool of labour to draw upon, and locally sourced provisions for their logging camps. Without these necessities, harvesting the immense stands of pine they coveted would be more expensive.

The government then decided to push the frontier of settled Canada West farther north. But how would this be accomplished? In essence, the government operated under the old maxim: build it and they will come. In the 1840s and 1850s, "colonization" roads were constructed northward from the settled south, opening the hinterlands to settlement. The Free Grant and Homestead Act of 1868 provided up to 80 hectares of land free for individuals 18 years or older with a family subject to certain conditions being met: the settler had to clear and cultivate six hectares and erect a suitable dwelling for habitation, reside on the lot at least six months of the year, and clear at least eight-tenths of a hectare per annum over a period of five years to obtain a deed for the land. Of course, such gifting of already occupied land to settlers for farming or resource extraction didn't take into account the entirely different Anishinaabeg view of nature and the physical environment, which is that they are shared, not "owned."

Lured by the offer of free plots, thousands of settlers packed up their worldly goods and headed north over the next half century. Inevitably, hamlets and villages appeared. Some succeeded, and thanks to modern tourism and the appeal of cottage living are as vibrant as ever. Many more failed, falling by the wayside and becoming ghost towns.

While all unsuccessful communities have their own tales, the common denominator in their extirpation was the land itself. When the region was initially opened for settlement, everyone was certain that under the dense forest canopy lay thick, rich loam that could sustain bountiful croplands. That was certainly the case in Europe. Instead, when the hoe hit the dirt, homesteaders, with few exceptions, found sandy or rock-strewn soil, and even this was spread only thinly over the impenetrable Canadian Shield. The land, simply put, was beyond productive cultivation.

But this book isn't about mourning the death of settlements. Rather, it's about chronicling their stories and the stories of those who bet their futures on them — pioneers in every sense of the word. There were challenges and heartbreak but also triumphs and inspiring examples of entrepreneurial spirit. Binding it all together was a sense of community that came from shared experience.

Every ghost town is worthy of remembrance, I believe, so how did I select these ones for inclusion in this book? One mandate I set for myself was to cover as much of the expanse of cottage country as possible, rather than focus on one region, as I did previously with *Ghost Towns of Muskoka*. I also wanted to ensure that the narratives were as varied as possible — to include not only farming hamlets settled largely by those of British descent but also a Georgian Bay port (Byng Inlet), a francophone community (Desaulniers), a lumber company town (Kiosk), and a settlement of Germanic immigrants (Germania).

 To Get There

For those who wish to visit these ghost towns for themselves, there are a few things to keep in mind. Many of the existing remnants are on private property. I've found most landowners to be hospitable and willing to grant permission to explore, so seek approval whenever possible, respect private property, and comply with any NO TRES-PASSING signs you encounter. It's also a good idea to have on hand up-to-date, detailed road maps of the areas you visit. Cellphone service may be spotty in certain regions.

PART ONE

Southern Cottage Country

HINDON HILL

(Township of Minden Hills, Haliburton County)

Tall and broad, William Toye wasn't afraid of hard work. Nor was he a stranger to it. His calloused hands told that tale. But whereas his body was strong, his spirit had been broken by the harsh, rocky landscape he'd been struggling to cultivate for the better part of two miserable decades. *I don't want to see any more of it*, he thought firmly, gazing upon the barren farm.

His mind had been made up. He'd be leaving. There was apprehension but also the twinkle of excitement at the prospect of taking up the government offer to move any willing families out of Hindon Hill and set them up on new land. William had jumped at it. The faster he could put the failed promise of the farm and the community behind him, the better. There would be no grieving, no tears shed. He wanted out.

And William wasn't alone. Hindon Hill had borne nothing but bitter fruits.

The rural hamlet of Hindon Hill was the social centre of sparsely settled Hindon Township and yet was tiny and hardscrabble at the best of times.

Today, a century after William Toye said goodbye, the former community has been almost completely swallowed up by encroaching forest. Were he alive, Toye wouldn't be saddened by its fate. But things didn't start out so badly. In fact, Hindon Hill was born of enthusiasm and hope.

Starting from the 1840s, there was immense and growing pressure on the colonial government to open what is now Haliburton County to settlement. With all the land in the southern part of the colony spoken for, people clamoured for cheap land where they could establish farms of their own. To them, Haliburton looked very enticing. There was also pressure from Britain to help relieve the stresses of the Irish Potato Famine and a rapidly growing population.

In 1846, the commissioner of Crown lands, Peter Vankoughnet, authorized a policy of settlement in Haliburton and Muskoka. A series of colonization roads would be built and title to land given free provided certain conditions were met. Vankoughnet was confident this would appease those demanding new lands, as well as help supply the many lumber camps operating in the area with foodstuffs and labour. The plan, of course, presupposed that the area was suitable for farming.

Many surveyors knew it wasn't. They reported that in many places "there was not enough soil to hold their [property boundary] stakes and that in others there was nothing but sand." In other words, the soil was anything but arable. But the fly wasn't yet in the ointment. As soon as it was announced that Haliburton was opening for settlement, eager throngs descended upon the county. Some came under their own initiative. Others were lured there by the Canadian Land and Emigration Company of London, which purchased a vast block of land the Crown Lands Department had advertised for sale in the hope that private enterprise would promote rapid settlement. Regardless of how they arrived, Haliburton was launched with an air of optimism.

Hindon Township, surveyed in 1860 and taking its name from a town in England, was no different. Although much of it wasn't surveyed for settlement, the southern half attracted land-hungry pioneers. What they found was, at least at first blush, attractive. "The land everywhere throughout the county is broken by hills, and the valleys between the hills form lakes filled with the purest and most pellucid water," observed Charles Pelham Mulvany, a Church of England clergyman and historian, in 1884. "The whole of the county, with the small portions cleared around the settlements, is covered with a dense forest, consisting chiefly of maple, birch, beech, basswood, and hemlock, and before the arrival of the lumberman there was a considerable amount of pine." It was nothing if not beautiful.

In the first decade, settlement was slow but steady. In 1869, the *Victoria County Directory* recorded a population of about 50 souls. Among the names were some that would long be associated with Hindon Hill, including the Taylors, Wrights, and Coulters. By 1880, that number had tripled. Despite hardships, the mood was buoyant — free land! — and a sense of community emerged.

James Toye, William's father, arrived during this period. Born in Ireland in 1845, he and his wife, Jane, came to Haliburton in 1873 to begin clearing land and build a cabin. Jane died in 1885, but James continued.

Like everyone else in Hindon Hill, James farmed as best he could. Potatoes and other root crops, grown in the thin soil and stored in root cellars or root houses (built into the side of a hill and covered with sand for insulation), provided the mainstay of one's diet. Every family kept large gardens to supply other vegetables, even if they might grow scraggly and stunted. Hogs were raised and butchered in the autumn, and every family fished and hunted to put regular protein on the table. Diets tended to be monotonous, and in some lean years, bordered on impoverishment.

Another early settler was Englishman Edward Aldred Austen. After a distinguished, decade-long career in the Royal Navy that saw him serve in the Crimean War aboard the 40-gun warship HMS *Arethusa*, Austen and his wife sailed for Canada and took up residence in London, Ontario, where he found work as a carpenter. Hungry for land of his own and seduced by government-produced literature extolling the virtues of the region, Austen decided to settle in Haliburton.

In the spring of 1876, Austen walked 482 kilometres north to claim his land in Hindon. He spent the summer there, building a cabin and clearing land before returning to London, again on foot, in the autumn. The following year, Edward and his wife and their young son, Albert, retraced his steps

Left: Built at a cost of $290, School Section (SS) No. 9 Stanhope opened in 1898 with Nellie Gilbard as teacher. After it closed in 1939, it was used as a cottage for many years and then fell into neglect. The school was purchased by the Minden Hills Museum in 1990 and moved there in 1994. After restoration, it was opened to the public in 1995.
Right: The interior of SS No. 9. During colder months, older children or the teacher would arrive at the schoolhouse early to start the fire and thaw the water and ink wells. Of particular interest in the recreated schoolhouse are the clock and exterior sign, both of which are original to SS No. 9.

and settled into their homestead. He couldn't have known it at the time, but Austen was establishing roots in Hindon Hill that would run deeper than almost any other family — his descendants lived on the farm until recent memory.

Thanks to the arrival of the Toyes and Austens and other families like them, enough people were now living on farms scratched from the soil around Hindon Hill that a school was required. About 1880, the first classes of School Section (SS) No. 9 were held in a log schoolhouse — very likely a former settler's cabin — at the head of Brady Lake (a large rock in the lake, known locally as Schoolhouse Rock, is just offshore of the school's one-time location). With no road access, children trudged along the shoreline or came by boat. Consequently, classes only ran from May to November.

Nonetheless, having a schoolhouse was a symbol of progress, and residents were proud of it.

Soon enough, the deficiencies of this schoolhouse became glaringly obvious. It was too remote, too small, and its roof leaked terribly. A new schoolhouse was needed. Widow Rachel Gannon (née Taylor) donated a parcel of the land (Lot 6, Concession A, Stanhope) that she and her husband, James, had settled in 1870, and a fine plank school was built in 1897. Blackboards covered three walls, and the teacher's desk sat at the front of the classroom. A potbellied stove stood in the centre; students who sat near it lamented that they were always too hot, while those far away complained of being too cold.

Teachers were young women, not much older than some of their students, who came from outside the area on one-year contracts for which they were paid (as of 1890) $16 per month. Their days were long and difficult. They woke early, pulled themselves from bed at the farmhouses where they boarded, and trudged to the school by 8:00 a.m. to light the stove. Lessons began at 9:00 a.m. Somehow the teachers had to juggle lessons for all ages over the course of the day. School was dismissed at 4:00 p.m., but the teachers had to remain behind to clean and ensure the stove fire was out. Then it was an often-long walk back to the farmhouses they boarded at. Little wonder most teachers lasted one year and then left; the long hours and loneliness would have been arduous.

The school was at the heart of Hindon Hill's social life. Since there was no church in the area, religious services were held there. So, too, were Christmas concerts — a highlight on the calendar — and box socials. Members of the local Orange Lodge held their meetings within its walls, as well. If one had to pinpoint a psychological heart for Hindon Hill, the school was it.

Another boon for settlers came in the form of a co-op cheese factory located on Lot 9, Concession 1, of Stanhope. A cheese factory seemed like a good idea; crops might grow poorly, but surely cows could graze and produce milk even in the highlands of Haliburton. Several Hindon Hill farmers were shareholders and invested in expanding their herds so that they might sell excess milk to the factory. Hugh Coulter was one; in 1890, we find that he made $10 from the endeavour, a not unnoteworthy amount in a time and place when hard currency was hard to come by.

That was a win for Hugh and Margaret (née Taylor) Coulter, but there had been losses in the years after they arrived as newlyweds in 1863. The most notable occurred in 1887. On May 16, 15-year-old Rachel Coulter led her five-year-old sister, Barbara, and seven-year-old cousin, John James Gannon (James and Rachel Gannon's son), to the shores of Brady Lake. There, they piled into a canoe and paddled away, perhaps heading to or from school — the details are uncertain. The canoe was either unsound and began to take on water, or else was swamped by large waves on a storm-tossed lake. In either case, the children paddled desperately for shore but lost the race. Not uncommon for the time, none could swim, at least not well enough to stay afloat with the heavy clothing they likely wore to ward off any spring chill. All three drowned. No burial site has ever been found, so it's possible the bodies were never recovered.

As was the case in so much of cottage country, settlers in Hindon Hill were sustained by logging companies that offered winter employment in the deep-wood camps. The valuable pine was largely gone by the end of the 19th century, but smaller-scale hardwood harvesting continued for decades.

As everywhere in cottage country, logging played a prominent role in the Hindon Hill economy. At first, large lumber companies swooped in to harvest the towering pine, providing winter employment for the earliest settlers. When the pine was exhausted and the large lumber concerns had moved on in search of new resources, attention fell on hardwood trees that previously had been of little interest. New companies, though smaller in scale, arrived in the wake left by the pine-logging interests. They established bush camps of their own throughout Hindon Township, offering desperately needed winter employment for local men.

Most of the harvested logs were shipped out to be cut in mills in the village of Minden or farther afield, but there were exceptions. Some lumber was manufactured in Hindon Hill at a small sawmill established on the shores of Brady Lake by Edward Austen around the turn of the 20th century. His son, James, assisted.

For the first three decades of Hindon Hill's existence, its residents had to travel to Peterson Corners for their mail, an inconvenience that often cost them the better part of a day's travel. By 1906, the community had grown enough to deserve a post office of its own, which officially opened on January 27 under Catherine Taylor.

The Taylor family were among the first wave to arrive in Hindon Hill. Irish-born Dan Taylor had appeared on the scene in 1871 and three years later married local lass Elizabeth Hamilton. Sadly, the young bride died a few years into their marriage. In 1881, Dan wedded Catherine, a Scottish woman all of 19, so that by 1906 the Taylor home was alive with 12 children. The additional income that came with the position of postmaster would have been welcomed, indeed. Catherine served as postmaster until her untimely death in 1919, age 57.

Minnie May Rivers, a daughter of John Michael Rivers and Mary Toye — and therefore the granddaughter of James Toye — recorded some of her memories growing up in Hindon Hill during the 1920s. Youthful joys from winters of yesteryear stood out in her recollections. "We children would go sleigh riding down the hills or go for walks on the crust in the bright moonlight over the fence," she recalled. "There were no roads ploughed then. We always had a nice driving horse and cutter. After Christmas everything was dead, all the men went back to the lumber camps, and we did not see them until the spring breakup in March."

But Minnie also took pains to mention the hard work of her mother in feeding and clothing an expansive family: "Mother was very clever. She could do anything she put her hand to. She spun yarn for all the neighbours, as well as sewing and making clothes for different families and her own 12 children, and she made the most wonderful butter preserves. The women in those days made everything. They couldn't go to the supermarkets and buy all the goods. To raise 12 children in those days was really some job."

Minnie might not have expressed how truly difficult it was to provide for a family in hardscrabble Hindon Hill. Her memories, perhaps viewed through the lens of a child's eye, gave equal measure to the joys as to the hardships of life in this backwater. Had she been able to ask her parents, a different impression would have emerged. People were bone-tired and despondent. It was a tough life.

By the 1920s, even the Ontario government began to realize the cruelty of promoting agricultural settlement in Hindon Township. Half a century of hardships had passed, with most settlers having nothing to show for their tireless labour. The provincial government offered those remaining the chance to leave for new lands in the Little Claybelt of the Temiskaming Region in Northern Ontario (known at the time as New Ontario).

"In return for the 80 or 100 acres of rocky farm land and scrub trees where some of them have spent the best part of their life in an effort to wrest a living from the grudging soil," wrote the *Toronto Daily Star* on September 15, 1927, "the settlers in question have accepted the government's offer of 80 acres of land in New Ontario, with an option on another 80, help in erecting new homes, and free transportation of all effects."

For many Hindon Hill families, the decision to take the government up on the offer was an easy one. They had been worn down over the years, their spirits broken by the false promise of the land and by the ceaseless toil ("years of a losing fight, years of just, with an almost superhuman effort, making both ends meet and the realization that in the end they would be broken," in the words of the *Daily Star* scribe). Accepting the offer represented "the end of a courageous struggle against odds."

Among those taking up the offer was 43-year-old William Toye. The father of 12 had been finding it increasingly difficult to put enough food on the table to feed his large family and to purchase even the most modest of luxuries. What little money he made was from felling sawlogs on his property, assisted by his 18-year-old daughter ("Stella is a cracker-good teamster," he proudly told the *Daily Star* reporter). But it was never enough. William was eager to leave.

When the *Daily Star* reporter asked him if he had any regrets, William's answer was quick in coming: "Not a darned bit. I have had a mighty tough time here and I'm glad to see the end of it…. I love farming and cattle and things, but this is too much, there is nothing to look forward to."

The only concession he made was that it was hard to leave friends and neighbours because they were "a mighty fine crowd." But, in truth, he'd see many of them again. His father, 81-year-old James Toye, and his mother were coming along. So, too, was his brother, Johnstone. Also heading north

William and Jennie Toye and their children, taken several years before they took up the offer of new land and a fresh start in the Temiskaming region. The hard life in Hindon Hill had worn down William: "This is too much," he dejectedly told a reporter.

were several neighbouring families: the Hewitts, the Trumbulls, and three Kent households headed by brothers Malcolm, James, and Oliver. Together they formed the nucleus of a new community near Kenogami, just west of Charlton.

But enough people stubbornly stayed behind to keep alive a semblance of community at Hindon Hill. The school and post office both endured for many years, serving a vastly reduced population.

Although school class sizes were far smaller, the important task of educating area youth remained. Indeed, it was only in the 1920s that full-year classes began to be offered, as opposed to the May to November terms of yesteryear. The school also remained the core of Hindon Hill's social life. That was why it came as such a blow when the decision was made to close SS No. 9 in 1939. Its loss was deeply felt by everyone.

As for the post office, after Catherine Taylor's death, the position of postmaster passed to Jennie Cameron for a few years before it fell under two long-serving women: Ruby MacKay from 1921 to 1938 and Elizabeth Coulter from 1939 to 1950, when the post office closed. Elizabeth and her husband, William, were among the handful of diehards who stubbornly clung to Hindon Hill even after the community was clearly well beyond its best-before date. Such was the sense of community even at this late date that people refused to move on from it. After all, neighbours were more than friends; in most cases, years of intermarriage had made them family.

The closure of the post office hammered home another nail in the hamlet's coffin. It had been the last amenity that gave the village some semblance of permanency. With it gone, Hindon Hill was no longer even officially a place on the map. In the eyes of Canada Post, and therefore the government, it was no more.

More than 70 years have gone by since then. The passage of time has ensured that Hindon Hill is well and truly gone. The reaper has done his work well. Those few who might have remembered Hindon Hill as a distinct community have passed on, taking with them oral history than can never be replaced. Homes and barns have been reduced to shells or foundations. Photos have curled and faded, and headstones in cemeteries have weathered under the relentless assault of rain and snow.

Hindon Hill is almost deathly silent today. Here and there one finds modern homes, and cottages dot the shores of Brady Lake. Relics of the pioneer-era settlement are harder to find, though certainly still there, shrouded by underbrush, hiding from a world they no longer recognize.

 To Get There

Hindon Hill lies on Brady Lake Road about one kilometre north of Highway 118. When driving down Brady Lake Road the distance is measured not in kilometres but in years, since this was originally part of the Bobcaygeon Colonization Road along which settlers travelled to take up their bush lots, brimming with hope for the future. In the regenerated forest along the way lies evidence of these shattered hopes in the form of ruined homesteads. For the best relic of Hindon Hill, point your car toward Minden. Minden Hills Museum and Heritage Village (mindenhills.ca/museum) boasts a fine collection of artifacts and almost a dozen pioneer-era buildings. Among a century-old bank, an 1860s settler's cabin, a cookhouse, and a church stands the former SS No. 9 Stanhope. Moved here in 1990 and beautifully restored, it serves as some comfort for descendants of the hardy families who settled Hindon Hill.

GERMANIA

(Town of Bracebridge, Muskoka District)

When Velda Gilbert passed away in 2014, she took with her 98 years of irreplaceable memories related to the hamlet of Germania, a community into which she was born and remained for most of her life. Velda had literally watched the village live and die.

Forests have swallowed up once-thriving farmsteads, and the decay of years has reduced buildings to rot and ruin, changing the landscape forever. And yet so much remained in Velda's vivid recollections. I had the good fortune of meeting and interviewing this kindly woman — warm and hospitable in a way found only in tiny communities — a few years before her passing with the intention of preserving some of the history she had watched unfold.

Velda was frail, barely 1.5 metres tall, and couldn't have weighed more than 40 kilograms. She insisted on showing me Germania's historic church, a point of great pride. With each shuffling step, she seemed to travel another year back in time, and a stream of stories tumbled from her mouth. Nearly blind, she nonetheless could clearly see the faces of friends and neighbours

Top: Settlers in Germania made full use of the resources of their forested lots, including making maple syrup each spring as a replacement for expensive store-bought white sugar. Julia Weis, a local woman who became one of the village school's most popular teachers, is second from the left lending a hand.

Left: Germania was a rarity in cottage country — an ethnic community composed, at least in its early years, almost entirely of settlers of German descent. It was a tightly knit community bonded by language, culture, blood, and marriage. Pictured is Christina Greb, born in Germania in 1889 to early Germanic homesteaders Wilhelm (William) and Hannah Greb.

long gone and was anxious that they be remembered. By the time we reached the steps of the church, she was back in an era of horse-drawn carriages, black-and-white photographs, and a Muskoka still very much in its infancy.

The story of Velda, and that of Germania itself, began in the early 1870s when a migration of German settlers took up land in this corner of Draper Township, began clearing land, and birthed Germania. The names of early families included Weis, Wettlaufer, Gilbert, Speicher, Weissmiller, Bourneman, and Kreb. These families, interconnected by marriage both in Germany and in Canada, form a thread of continuity in the village's history and are notable for their varied contributions.

Velda's grandparents, Wilhelm (William) and Margaretha (Margaret) Gilbert, were among the first to settle Germania. Hailing from Hesse-Darmstadt, Germany, where they were born in 1839 and 1848, respectively, they fled economic hardships for a new start in the recently opened Muskoka District. Accompanying them was William's younger brother, Georj (George), and his wife, Katherina, and Katherina's parents, Herman and Maria Dorothea Weissmuller.

William and George established farms across the road from each other at what became the heart of the community. Carving homesteads from the dense forests was difficult work, but they persevered, and their toil eventually paid off with rich fields of wheat, oats, and beans.

Herman Weissmuller, however, had other plans in mind. Born in 1816, he was already a weathered man in his fifties when he, his wife, Maria Dorothea, and their nine children arrived in Canada. Although he farmed enough to get by, Herman pinned his hopes on the sawmill he established on the shores of Weissmuller, or Germania, Lake. Finished lumber was transported by wagon to Kielty's Siding at South Falls, where it was loaded onto railway flatcars and shipped to urban centres in Southern Ontario and the United States. The Weissmuller Lumber Company employed half a dozen men year-round and even more in the winter, when men with strong backs were needed in bush camps to harvest timber.

In 1875, even as the farmers were still struggling to tame the land, the first steps toward establishing a church were made. A board of trustees was established, comprising the three most prominent names in the community:

This photograph provides some hint of the challenges settlers faced upon first arriving at their lots. The heavily forested land had to be cleared of trees and underbrush to make way for a home, a barn, pasture lands, and fields to grow crops. It was a Herculean task made worse by the swarms of blackflies and mosquitoes that plagued them at every turn.

George Gilbert, Herman Weissmuller, and Nikolaus Wettlaufer. It fell to them to organize the building efforts, raise the necessary funds, and acquire land.

In most 19th-century communities, local landholders donated small parcels of land, generally two-tenths of a hectare or so, upon which to build a church. Germania was no different. It was William Gilbert — Velda's grandfather — who stepped forward to sign over a lot, and as a result, the church became unofficially known as Gilbert Lutheran Church in his honour. Herman Weissmuller did his part by donating the necessary lumber from his sawmill. Construction began in 1876, and by the next year, the church was ready for services. Building the church was a community affair but so, too, was maintaining it — all parishioners owning farmland were required to supply just under a cubic metre of wood per year for heating.

To provide a home for the minister, a parsonage was constructed opposite the church on the northwest corner of the village intersection. This meant that for a time the community enjoyed the presence of a resident minister, a luxury few hamlets could claim. But after the parsonage burned down sometime around 1885, Germania was forced to share its preacher with nearby Gravenhurst. Residents were required to provide the minister with accommodations when he was tending to affairs in the village, as well as transportation to and from Gravenhurst.

In keeping with the community's ethnic composition, church services were initially held in both English and German. This practice continued until nearly the turn of the century, by which time a new generation of Canadian-born and fluently English-speaking residents began to take over communal affairs. Concurrently, Germania's ethnic makeup was changed when several non-German families arrived to add diversity to the community. Henceforth, services were held in English.

On September 1, 1884, after vigorous campaigning by Herman Weissmuller, Germania was granted a post office. Weissmuller's son, John, was named postmaster, and the post office operated out of the Weissmuller home. John remained involved with the post office for less than a year. William Stamp assumed the role of postmaster in July 1885 and moved its operation to his home.

No pioneer farming community would be complete without a blacksmith. While shoeing horses may have been the most important part of his job description, it was far from the only task a blacksmith performed. He could make nails and wrought-iron cooking ware, mend a harrow or plough, and forge tools and hinges. Rough roads quickly wore down the iron rims on wooden wagon wheels, requiring repair. Many blacksmiths even made repairs on the wagons themselves. In Germania's case, the man pumping the bellows and hammering upon the anvil was Nicholas (Nick) Weis.

Born on October 27, 1870, Nick was the son of John and Caroline Weis. Instead of following his father into farming, Nick elected to take up blacksmithing. After a time away apprenticing, he returned to Germania in the early 1890s and set up a smithy on the corner of his parents' farm facing the road and almost directly opposite the school. Quiet and friendly, Nick was a beloved member of the community. Children delighted in watching him at work and often stopped at his shop after school to witness metal being hammered into shape.

If Caroline Weis had had her way, however, the family would never have been in Germania in the first place. Caroline, who descended from Polish aristocracy that had fallen on hard times, had married John in New York State, and together they had built a fine home and farm in Dunkirk on the south shore of Lake Erie. Caroline had resisted when her husband voiced his intention of uprooting the family and moving to Muskoka. Why move when they had it good? But John was insistent. Upon arriving in Muskoka, Caroline's heart sank like a stone in a pool of water. There was nothing but bush and rock. She hated everything on their new homestead, so much so that she kept her good dishes packed in a barrel for more than six months, hoping beyond hope that they would go back to New York and resume their previous life.

Of course, John and Caroline never did leave, and Germania was better for their presence. They helped to build a village that by the turn of the century was feeling good about itself. It boasted a growing population, a thriving sawmill, a blacksmith, a post office, a well-attended school, and a beautiful church. Farms were thriving.

One of the more prosperous farms belonged to John Weis. His grand-daughter, Mary Fitzmaurice, was proud and a bit awed by his success in cultivating the land. "Grandpa wanted to plant strawberries," she told me. "Everyone said they would never grow, since Muskoka had killing frosts even in June, but he went ahead and planted a huge field, anyway. There were no weather reports to go by, but he seemed to know when a storm or frost was coming and would call on everybody to help him cover the field with straw, rags, and paper. His strawberries thrived."

Mary continued. "The same with the fruit orchard he planted. No one had fruit trees growing around here, but he planted two each of peach, pear, plum, cherry, and apple trees. When the temperature dropped low, he would build smug fires among the trees, and it helped save the crops."

The Gilberts' farm was just as bountiful. When William Gilbert died in 1896, he left the homestead to his son, Henry, and daughter-in-law, Rachel. Velda, born in 1916, was the couple's second child. During our conversation, Velda pointed toward her childhood home opposite the church and spread her arms wide. "All of this," she said, indicating land now heavily forested, "was once fields of wheat and oats and beans. Daddy did all the ploughing by hand and never once complained. We had 30 head of cattle for milking, and my father raised calves up and sold them. The oats went to feed them. Wheat went to the chickens. My brothers, Lawrence and Bob, helped with the animals, while we girls — me and my sister, Eileen — helped Mom around the house. We were brought up to work."

And, of course, the Weises and Gilberts were far from unique. There were perhaps two dozen other farms in the area, pushing the bush back as much as a kilometre and a half from the roads and replacing the trees with huge fields of grain and pasture.

Germania continued to grow and prosper in the new century. In 1906, after more than 20 years, William Stamp retired as postmaster and handed over his duties to Julius Rossgar (often anglicized as Rusker). The new appointee was an ambitious individual, a man who had visions of prospering as a merchant. To that end, he opened a combined post office and general store — the first in Germania — along the shores of Weissmuller Lake. To residents of the little farming community, the store's opening was an exciting development. After only three years, Rossgar sold the store to Willis and Mary Couke, and it was under their ownership that the store operated for the greater balance of the community's existence.

The early days of the 20th century were arguably the heyday of the Germania Nazareth Evangelical Lutheran Church. Attendance was at a peak, beautiful new floors were laid throughout, and Charlie Speicher, a gifted local musician, donated a "mouse-proof" organ worth $40. The church was the beating heart of the community, and it showed in the attention parishioners lavished upon it even while the substandard soil was providing little in the way of profitable harvests.

No one in Germania at the time would have guessed that within a few generations the community would wither away. There was no dramatic event that spelled the doom of Germania as a community. Instead, it was just a slow sagging of fortunes that played out over half a century.

With a few exceptions, life in Germania in the 1910s, 1920s, and 1930s was peaceful and slow-moving. Children walked several kilometres to school each day, their numbers growing as they approached Germania. The church remained the centre of social life. Homesteads were passed on to a second generation. Tractors and cars were luxuries afforded to people in seemingly distant places; horses remained the means of transportation and farm labour. Life carried on much as it always had.

But change was afoot. It began in 1919 when Willis Couke died, leaving Mary to manage their store on her own. Four years later, she sold the property, and the new owners closed the shop. The nearest store of any consequence was in Bracebridge, which one visited infrequently at best. "Dad would hitch up the horse and buggy once every few weeks," recalled Velda Gilbert. "Sometimes I'd go with my parents. Sitting there, we'd be near freezing on cold winter days. But it was exciting going to town. Days I didn't go were anxious. I couldn't wait for Daddy to come home to see if he brought any candy." Velda laughed at the memory even as her eyes grew moist with the recollection of her beloved father. The tone in her voice was clear. Even almost a century later, she was still proudly "Daddy's little girl."

A peddler offered an alternative to going to town. He travelled to the different homes in a truck laden with groceries for families to buy. In turn, he bought the farmers' milk and cheese. In general, farms were self-sufficient, and families produced most of their needs.

The Weissmuller mill closed around the same time as the store but under more dramatic circumstances. Herman Weissmuller had died in 1905, but the business continued under the guidance of his children. One day, about two decades after Herman's death, the mill burned to the ground. After taking stock, the Weissmullers decided against rebuilding and instead moved to greener pastures in Bala. Meanwhile, the Speicher family purchased the blackened steam engine and removed it to their own property, where a new mill was erected. That mill would burn down, as well, drawing a curtain on the lumber industry in Germania.

The horse and wagon remained the principal means of transportation, ensuring a steady demand for the blacksmith's services. Nonetheless, Nick Weis saw the writing on the wall — automobiles were the future and Germania the past. Around 1930, he moved to Toronto to become a homebuilder. No one took up his mantle as blacksmith and the building stood empty. Local children often played in the abandoned shop with its silent forge.

Young Janice Wiser plays with her puppies, blissfully oblivious to the tragedy that had befallen her family a few years prior with the shooting death of her brother Harold. Janice had a tough childhood — she lost her father at a young age and only gained a grade six education because she had to walk eight kilometres through woods to reach school, often missing class when the snow was piled high.

For most children, school was a privilege. Farm work took precedence, and most boys left school around the age of 12 to begin working at logging camps. The experience of Janice Christina Wiser was, if not entirely typical, illustrative of the difficulties area children had in obtaining a sound education. "Mom had to walk five miles through the bush to get to school," explained Gayle MacDonald. "It wasn't so bad when her older brother, Bernal, five years her senior, accompanied her, but he left to work in camps at age 12, leaving Mom to make that trek by herself. Mom often missed school during the winter because of bad weather, and when she did get there and the weather turned, she would spend the night with the teacher. Because of all the missed school due to inclement weather, Mom only made it through grade six."

Gayle continued. "One time she was late for school because she encountered a bear along the way and had to sit quietly for it to move on. When she told everyone at school about the bear, they laughed at her and said she made it up to avoid a reprimand for being late. She was vindicated a few days later when others encountered the bear in the same bush."

It would have been hard to reprimand Janice at any rate. She and her family had endured so much. On December 17, 1933, two years before she was born, 14-year-old Harold Wiser went into the bush with farmhand Norman Ruttan to shoot some foxes or hares. Harold had desperately wanted furs that he could sell to buy a Christmas present for his baby brother, Bernal. Under mysterious circumstances, Harold was shot in the head by Ruttan and died shortly thereafter. More pain followed for the family. Less than a decade later, in 1941, Harold and Janice's father, Herbert, died of stomach cancer. Janice was only five years old at the time; the only memories she had of her father were of a sick man who spent most of his time in bed.

Mary Fitzmaurice grew up in the stagnant Germania of the 1930s. "Most people in Germania still farmed at the time," she recalled. "We lived on a farm, too, but my dad hated farming and he hated horses. Any farming was done very reluctantly." Mary laughed frequently as we chatted about her childhood. "Dad mostly worked in mills. He loved machinery. He once bought the engine from a burned-out sawmill and had a heyday using it to power all sorts of machinery and make things. We had new skis every time we grew an inch, just to give him an excuse to use his engine."

Mary's mother supplemented the family income by serving as village postmaster for a few years in the late 1930s and early 1940s. "Mother ran the post office until a cyclone passed through our farm one day," said Mary, her mind travelling back to the 1940s. "Our neighbour watched it from her home. The cyclone cut a path through the water, destroying our pigpen, going around the barn and tossing the chicken pen into that neighbour's field and then it went around the house and destroyed our woodshed before heading off into the bush. My mother insisted that was God telling us to move off the farm and we did."

Many others followed the Fitzmaurices' lead; there was an exodus from farms in the postwar period. By the 1950s, the once-proud village was a withered shadow of its former self, home to but a fraction of the number living there just half a century prior. Rural delivery saw the closure of village post offices — Germania's shutting on November 30, 1957. At the same time, centralized schooling spelled the demise of the one-room schoolhouse. The end for Germania's came in 1960, after which time children were bused to Bracebridge, leaving the old school empty and ignored.

As the population shrank, the church began to suffer for lack of resources and attention. Indeed, there is a very good chance it would have shared the fate of the nearby schoolhouse, which recently collapsed under the weight of snow and years of neglect, if not for the tireless devotion of Godfrey Clark.

Clark grew up on a farm 13 kilometres away in Housey's Rapids, and as a child in the 1950s, he and his family attended the church. His mother, Jessica Speicher, a descendant of one of Germania's founding families, was proud of her family's deep ties to the church and the fact that her uncle had donated the organ. Since his retirement, Clark has faithfully devoted his

William Gilbert donated land for the Germania Lutheran Church in 1875, with construction taking place the following year. For a time, the community enjoyed the luxury of a local parish priest. At first, services were held in German, but over time English was adopted. Today, 150 years after opening, the church stands as a reminder of Germania's past.

time to preserving the church: he handles the finances, oversees maintenance, and performs many repairs himself. "Caring for the church is a way of honouring my mother," he said, emotion tinging his voice. "I'm deeply rooted in religion, and my roots are bound to this church."

It's easy to feel the church's pull. The dull grey siding that once covered its exterior walls has been removed to reveal the sturdy timber of the original construction, the logs seeming to symbolize the strength and indomitable spirit of those who settled this difficult landscape. The interior, which hasn't been altered much over the years, breathes the atmosphere of a bygone era. The pews, altar, baptismal font, and oil lamps are all original, and the century-old organ is still there. Heating is provided solely by an ancient wood stove. The original land grant, issued on February 1, 1875, hangs encased in glass on a wall.

The cemetery adjacent to the building gives silent testimony to the many German families that once populated this part of Draper. Reading the inscriptions on the stones, one begins to comprehend how tightly knit the community was. Neighbours weren't just friends; they were quite literally family, either through blood or marriage.

When Velda led me among the fading and cracked tombstones that spring day 20 years ago, her mind began to travel decades into the past. Despite failing eyesight, she was able to point out by memory the graves of friends and relatives who had left her.

One of the stones, the tallest in the cemetery, is a cross-shaped memorial to Adam and Wilhelmina Dietz. Velda shared that the Dietzes were well-respected farmers who came to Germania in the 1890s. She then raised one of her rail-thin hands, crooked a finger, and beckoned me to follow. We walked to the far rear of the cemetery, Velda leaning on my arm as the ground grew uneven and we pushed our way through foliage. Just outside the cemetery boundaries, she pointed, guiding my eyes to a small grave marker partly obscured by leaves. This was a grave the parishioners had wanted to forget about.

The grave belonged to Katherine Dietz, daughter of Adam and Wilhelmina. Hers is a tragic story. Two years after her mother died in 1901, the 29-year-old became pregnant out of wedlock. Her courter abandoned

This graveyard is dotted with headstones belonging to generations of Germania's families. And then there's the lonely grave of Katherine Dietz, buried alone just outside the cemetery proper. Unwed and with child, she committed suicide in 1903.

her, her father was ashamed of her, and the community shunned her. Despondent and alone, she ended her misery by walking into Weissmuller Lake, allowing the weight of her sodden dress to drag her to the bottom. Guilty now of two transgressions against the morals of the day — pregnancy before marriage and suicide — Katherine was buried outside the cemetery property on unconsecrated ground.

Were she still alive today, Velda would undoubtedly be happy to hear that services continue to be held in her beloved church in the summer, once a month in July and August, and are well-attended by people cognizant of the history the building represents.

The church is one of the few original structures still standing. Germania — the village of yesteryear, not the collection of modern homes that occupy some of the pioneer lots — is now all but forgotten. Directly across from the cemetery, a blue early-20th-century home marks the Gilbert farm. Elsewhere, former concession roads leading to bush farms are

When William Gilbert died in 1896, he left the homestead to his son, Henry, and daughter-in-law, Rachel. The Gilberts had a dairy herd of 30 cows — large for Muskoka — and extensive fields of wheat, oats, and beans. The farmhouse still stands and remains a residence to this day.

overgrown and often barely visible. Along these roads, one finds occasional hints of the farms of yesteryear — a fence post here, a lilac bush there. Until recently, the schoolhouse stood, as well, but age and neglect saw its roof collapse under a heavy load of snow. Some postwar playground equipment remains in the yard where once children played during recess.

To Get There

Germania lies east of Bracebridge and south of Highway 118 along Germania Road. It's a bit of a winding route; at one point, Germania Road turns east, while the way continues south as Waters Road. The one-time hamlet is huddled around a T-intersection where Germania Road jags south once again. The church and cemetery are on the southeast corner. Across is the former Gilbert homestead. On the southwest corner are the remnants of the school. Weissmuller Lake is farther south along Germania Road.

3

UFFINGTON

(Town of Bracebridge, Muskoka District)

I n 2009, a handful of former congregants gathered at St. Paul's Anglican Church to say one last farewell. The church, built in 1889, had been part of Uffington since its early days and had come to represent one of the few tangible reminders of the faded community. Apprehension feathered through their stomachs; all knew what was soon to happen. The crowd was quiet, the same muffled silence experienced at a funeral. Tears welled in eyes and lumps formed in throats as the machinery clattered toward the historic structure. Some turned away before the walls were pulled down; others stoically watched the spectacle to the very end.

Everyone knew there was no going back to better times when the church pews were filled to overflowing and the village hummed with energy. But it still hurt. The demise of the church in many ways echoed the fate of its community. Both were now gone forever.

While people still reside there, the Uffington of today pales in comparison with that of its heyday a century ago, when it boasted a population of several hundred, the din of thriving commercial activity filled the air, and a steady stream of traffic passed along busy Peterson Road. Uffington was a large and recognizable community, not merely a collection of country homes as it is today.

The village was a crossroads like so many across pioneer-era Ontario, owing much of its importance to its position astride a busy thoroughfare. But it was unique in one key respect: whereas most crossroads communities cluster around a single intersection, Uffington huddled around two. These twin crossroads — Hawn and Peterson Roads in the west, Uffington and Peterson Roads in the east — formed bookends between which lay most of the village.

The community got its start in the 1860s when a handful of resolute pioneers pushed into the tangles of Draper Township to settle homesteads. These early settlers blazed the way for the wave of would-be homesteaders

In 1852, James Bridgland began the task of surveying Muskoka District. His report, written in January 1853, concluded that the region was barren and unpromising for agriculture. It was ignored. Luck was on Uffington's side — it prospered. The soil here is marginally better for farming than most places in Muskoka. Also, it had plenty of lumber resources and, most importantly, straddled two busy crossroads — Hawn and Peterson Roads in the west and Uffington and Peterson Roads in the east — bringing commerce.

who flocked into the area over the following decades. Life was difficult in those early days. "The wife guarded the home against wild beasts while the young husband wielded the axe against the mighty pine," read the obituary of Phoebe Bull Matthews, who arrived in 1862.

Slowly, a community began to emerge. In 1864, Andrew Thompson campaigned for a post office serving Draper Township, naturally with himself as postmaster. He argued that its central location within the township and the fact that it sat astride busy Peterson Road made Uffington the perfect place for such a post office. The government agreed: on October 1, 1864, the Uffington post office officially came into existence operating out of Thompson's home. When Thompson left Uffington in 1872, John Doherty stepped in to fill the void. He was already a prominent man about town, serving as treasurer of Draper Township and president of the Uffington Agricultural Fair.

Robert McMurray opened the village's first store. From the shop's porch, he watched as several stagecoaches and numerous wagons rattled through town every day. Recognizing that their weary travellers and even more exhausted horses needed respite, McMurray opened a hotel, then used his wealth and prominence in local affairs to get himself elected as the first reeve of Draper Township.

McMurray's store wasn't the only one in town. George Spence arrived in Uffington in 1872, fresh off the boat from Ireland. A few years later, his farm on steady footing, Spence opened a shop of his own. And like McMurray before him, he, too, became township reeve. In 1889, Spence was made postmaster and the post office moved into his store — for the first time ever, residents could enjoy the convenience of shopping and picking up mail at the same time.

And that was just the beginning: more than a dozen other businesses appeared to transform Uffington into the economic heart of Draper Township. Uffington's good fortune was tied to its location astride Peterson Road and two busy secondary thoroughfares and to the lumbering taking place in the forests around it.

But Uffington was blessed in other ways, as well. The land there is one of the few patches of decent farmland in Muskoka — not great, but at least

A local sporting team — soccer, by the look of it — in 1930s Uffington. As the largest and most prosperous community in Draper Township, Uffington boasted luxuries that many smaller villages couldn't, including an agricultural society with seasonal fairs, many communal organizations (for example, a drama club), and sporting teams.

not all granite — meaning farmers weren't fighting a daily life-and-death struggle for survival. This relative comfort allowed them to devote time and resources to communal functions, such as founding an agricultural society, hosting seasonal fairs, and establishing fraternal organizations that collectively enriched the village.

Uffington was one of only seven villages in Muskoka that boasted a Loyal Orange Lodge, and its people were proud of the distinction. A fraternal organization consisting of patriotic Protestants, the Loyal Orange Lodge played a prominent role in the political and social life of any community that had one. Typically, lodges included among their membership some of the wealthiest and most important men in their respective communities, and as a result, they wielded considerable influence.

Loyal Orange Lodge (LOL) 634 was initiated on March 16, 1868, by a dozen men from Draper Township. Initially, lodge members met in a rented hotel room, but Timothy Patterson, a wealthy farmer and cattle breeder, took it upon himself to spearhead efforts to build a dedicated Orange Hall. Members donated funds, and James Smith offered a piece of land on the

Class from School Section (SS) No. 3 Draper. The school had a long and colourful history. It began in a settler's cabin, shared quarters with the local Loyal Orange Order, had a front-row seat in a tussle between the lodge and property owner James Smith, and then was burned out under mysterious circumstances. Nonetheless, the school endured, only closing in 1957.

northwest corner of the Peterson Road–Uffington Road crossroads upon which to build. Work began in August 1871 and was completed by the following spring. The first meeting of LOL 634 in its new home was on May 13, 1872.

A school was opened the same year that LOL 634 was started; the two would be intertwined in unexpected and dramatic ways. Classes were initially held in a log building beside the Orangemen's Lodge. Almost certainly, it was James Smith's original settler's shanty. Cold and damp, the building was less than ideal, but it had to do for the time being. By 1872, the deficiencies in the original school had become glaring, so trustees desperately searched for a place where classes could be held in greater comfort. The Loyal Orange Lodge offered use of its hall — most were parents, after all — for $8 every term, and school trustees enthusiastically agreed.

That was when things got interesting. Within a few years, James Smith had a falling out with the lodge, the nature of which is unrecorded. In rancour, he pointed out that the hall was sitting on private land — his, to be precise. There had never been anything more than a gentleman's agreement between Smith and the lodge for use of the property, and consequently the Orangemen were evicted. The hall was then handed over to the school board for its sole use. Hard feelings had barely subsided when the object of the controversy burned to the ground in 1877. There were some whispered accusations that a disgruntled Orangeman had taken his vengeance, but we'll never know the truth.

Now both students and Orangemen were homeless. A new schoolhouse was erected on the same lot and opened for classes in 1878. As for the Loyal Orange Lodge, it raised a new hall on a lot on the southeast corner of the crossroads that Matthew Patterson agreed to sell them for $1. This time, just to be certain, the lodge had a proper deed drawn up and signed.

Every village of any size had a blacksmith. Uffington was blessed with two at the same time: both Adam Chamber and Lorenzo Johnson opened shops in 1882. Chamber lasted about a decade, ultimately moving to Port Carling and greater success. Johnson lasted far longer. Born in England but

Born in 1848 and arriving in Muskoka around 1881 with his wife, Elizabeth, John Pascall (right) was a farmer and blacksmith. Pascall's son, John Junior (left), known as Jack to avoid confusion, followed his father into the trade and eventually opened his own shop in Utterson.

raised in the United States, he came to Canada in the late 1870s and spent several years as a blacksmith in Grimsby, on Lake Ontario. Newly wed, he headed for Muskoka and the promise of free land. Johnson worked the forge nearly until his death at the age of 73 in 1913.

John Pascall was the next blacksmith on the scene. Born in England in 1848, he came to Muskoka around 1881 with his wife, Elizabeth, where he farmed and opened a blacksmith shop. Smithing must have paid off, because in 1897, Pascall was forced to build a larger shop to keep up with the increase in business. John's son, John Junior, known as Jack, worked with him for several years before moving to Utterson to open a smithy of his own. Like Johnson, Pascall Senior worked hammer and forge right up till the end, dying on December 20, 1918.

Beyond the hotels, stores, and blacksmith shops, Uffington's businesses included a sawmill, a shoe shop run by Richard Ketching, two carpenters, a small confectionery and stationery store owned by Henry Buebler, and William Troskiss's pump-making shop. A stagecoach running between Uffington and Gravenhurst twice daily was operated by John Coulson, and after him by George Foster. There were three churches — Anglican, Presbyterian, Methodist — and a township hall. The population as of 1890, when Uffington was probably at its peak, stood at around 200, making it the largest rural community in Draper, Macauley, Stephenson, and Ryde Townships.

Uffington was a thriving community, but it hadn't come easily. There were hardships along the way, of course, and tragedies. The Toye family, headed by Frederick Nowell Toye, suffered more than most. In 1888, Frederick seemed to have it all — a loving wife and partner in Annie, five children (one happily married, four still at home), a successful farm, and the respect of neighbours that saw him named clerk of Draper Township. Heavy rain occurred on May 28, and when it stopped, the blackflies came out in maddening droves. To combat the bloodthirsty insects, a smudge fire was lit. When the family retired to their beds, they thought they'd put out the smudge.

The house caught fire later that evening. Seventeen-year-old Mary Bella, up late studying to be a teacher, was the first to become aware of the danger. She called to her parents, then ran from the house to summon help from neighbours. When she returned, she found the home engulfed in flames. Her family had perished in the fire. Annie's charred body was found protectively cradling her two youngest, one in each arm, in a futile effort to shield them from the flames. Thirteen-year-old William was still in his bed. Frederick was found on the ground floor — it appeared as if he'd run to the well with two pails, then turned back to save his family. The heartbreaking tragedy shook the community.

There was plenty more drama in Uffington, courtesy of the seasonal shantymen employed in area logging camps who had the unfortunate tendency to drink too much when patronizing the hotels' barrooms. Sometimes the drinking got out of hand and the booze-soaked antics escalated from boisterous revelry to something far darker.

McMurray's hotel often hosted exhibits for the fall fair — mostly preserves, baked goods, and handicrafts — in the upper rooms. Women had to pass by the barroom and the drunken louts revelling there. One night, the hotel was full of men whose manners — assuming they had any — had

Mat Watson (at left in a Gravenhurst hotel) was a Draper Township legend. A man of indescribable courage and strength, with a chivalrous streak a kilometre wide, he engaged in several tussles with drunken ruffians. One brawl, in defence of women and children, saw him square off against five louts — and win!

been drowned by whiskey. These men began to intimidate the women in the exhibit rooms, essentially holding them hostage. Mrs. McMurray asked the men to make way, but they refused. She asked again, more forcefully, but was told to make herself scarce.

Entering the picture at this point was local farmer Mat Watson. He didn't ask the drunkards to make way; he told them to and backed it up with his fists, which led to a fierce brawl between Watson and five glassy-eyed louts. Incredibly, when tempers had cooled and the punches had stopped, it was Watson who still stood. The gentleman then escorted the women to the exit, cementing for himself a reputation as the toughest and most chivalrous man in Draper Township.

Similar acts of drunken disorderliness plagued Uffington's second hotel, built around 1879 by William Briggs at the east end of town at the intersection of Uffington and Peterson Roads. One blustery winter night, a small gathering of patrons huddled near the fireplace to ward off the bone-gnawing chill. At one table sat three shantymen who grew rowdier with each shot of whiskey. When they began abusing the other patrons, Briggs refused to serve them further and ordered them out of his establishment.

They left but didn't go far. Instead, the enraged and embarrassed shantymen waited in the darkness for the other patrons to leave. Then then revealed themselves by cursing Briggs and throwing a rock through the window. Briggs rushed outside to drive them off. One of the ruffians, a troublemaker named John Dougherty, stabbed him three times in the chest with a knife. Briggs collapsed, his blood staining the snow crimson, and yet Dougherty continued his ruthless assault, stabbing the helpless victim three more times in the back. Amazingly, Briggs survived.

The hotels were caught in a quandary. Loggers were undeniably good for business, but they also brought with them bad behaviour, even violence. Both Briggs and McMurray struggled with the dilemma. In the end, the decision was taken out of their hands. As the timber became depleted in the 1890s, logging interests pulled up stakes and went farther north in search of untapped tracts of trees, taking the shantymen and their antics with them.

The turn of the century marked the beginning of a troubling era for Uffington. As the hoteliers predicted, in the absence of shantymen, their

As in all early Muskoka communities, Uffington saw its fortunes tied to the lumber trade. Winter logging meant seasonal jobs for farmers, a market for local produce, and clientele for hotel bars in the form of lumberjacks.

establishments suffered. The loss of the logging industry was felt throughout the community as employment was lost and revenue disappeared. Trains struck another blow against Uffington. The railways passed the village by, electing to run their north-south lines through Bracebridge and Gravenhurst to the west. This was a devastating gut punch to Uffington, as trains reduced road traffic along Peterson Road considerably, depriving the community of its lifeblood.

With empty barrooms and reduced traffic along Peterson Road, hotels couldn't survive, and neither remained open long into the twentieth century. Other business fared little better. Businessmen and farmers alike, men who just a few years before had looked to the future with confidence, certain that Uffington was on the verge of greatness, became despondent at the village's sagging fortunes and moved on. George Spence, a man who many thought symbolized Uffington and its promise, threw up his hands in 1899 and moved to Tillsonburg to open a new store. Most who fled went west to the Prairies.

A raging forest fire in 1913 devastated the reeling community, finishing the job begun by the loss of the logging industry and the evaporation of traffic along Peterson Road. August was unnaturally hot and dry that year. Forest and field alike were essentially tinder. As a result, a fire that began in Oakley Township soon spread out of control. Fanned by high winds, the inferno raced west into Draper Township. Uffington sat directly in its path.

Vina Bentley was a child at the time of the fire and remembered it with chilling vividness in her old age. She and her two siblings — Thomas and Matilda — were left with Mrs. Harry Bonnis, a neighbour, while her parents did what they could to keep the fire at bay. With flames seemingly all around, Mrs. Bonnis herded the Bentley children and her own seven offspring into the middle of a green meadow, the only fragile sanctuary she could find. "Tom and I carried water from a small creek with a pail and Mrs. Bonnis would sprinkle the grass around us," Vina recalled. "Her baby was nine months old. All we had to eat was a little milk. Mrs. Bonnis milked from a cow in a teapot."

Vina's father, a trustee, raced to the school to help rescue it. Her mother, meanwhile, tried to save the family home. "She put bedding and clothes down one well," Vina remembered, "but the boards caught fire and burned everything we had. Hens, geese, and pigs burned. Some of the cows were saved who stayed around the meadow."

At one point, with flames closing in on her, Vina's mother sought refuge by climbing down another well. She dipped her shoe in water and poured it over her head to keep her hair from catching fire. Periodically, she poked her head out to breathe fresh air before the heat chased her back down the well. Miraculously, she survived.

After fighting the fire for several days, the exhausted and soot-blackened residents of Draper broke down in tears as rain fell in sheets from the sky on August 22. "It was with hearts filled with gratitude to the giver of all good things that the people in our village watched the downpour of rain on Friday," noted the local correspondent in the *Muskoka Herald* on August 28, 1913, "which quenched the fire that for so many days had threatened the destruction of our homes."

No one died, thankfully, but 13 families were burned out by the conflagration, the Bentleys among them. Most — Vina's parents included — chose to leave the fading village for a fresh start elsewhere. Uffington became increasingly quiet with each passing year. Business owners faced the hard truth and began closing shop.

Through much of this period, the mail was carried by Henry Buckler. A colourful character, Buckler was a taxidermist and photo studio operator by trade. With increasingly less call for such services in the atrophying village, Buckler took on the role of postmaster in 1908. In the end, he served in this role for longer than anyone, only retiring in 1928 at the age of 68. By then, the only businesses remaining in Uffington were the store run by Samuel Hawn, who took over as postmaster, and a blacksmith shop, then operated by Jacob Matthias from nearby Matthiasville.

The transition from horse to machine on the farm, in the lumber woods, and even along the rural roads was a gradual one and therefore there was a continued need for Matthias's services for many years yet. In fact, the forge didn't cool until 1955. The store remained open a year beyond that, and then in 1957, the school closed, its single room silent for the first time in 79 years. By that time, the thriving village of yesteryear existed only in the memories of old-timers.

And yet the Loyal Orange Lodge endured until the 1990s, when there were still three members on the roll. "We didn't want it to end, but there weren't enough of us to keep it going, either," remembered William Allen, one of the last of Uffington's Orangemen. "There must be at least four members in a lodge, and when we didn't have that, we were forced to close. It was a real shame."

Thanks to proximity to Bracebridge and Highway 11, modern homes have appeared on one-time pioneer lots, restoring a semblance of life to the moribund community. But old Uffington, the village of yore, is fading. Farm fields are overgrown, barns have collapsed into piles of timber, and those who recall Uffington as a distinct community are becoming increasingly rare.

Some remnants of old Uffington continue to cling to life. Although weathered and dilapidated, the Orange Hall still stands across from a cemetery where many past members of the society lie buried. Elsewhere, the one-time Hawn store is a private residence. So, too, is the third and final School Section (SS) No. 3, now more than 130 years old. St. Paul's Anglican

Church stood until recent years. After being deconsecrated and torn down, all that was left were the handful of remaining headstones in the adjacent graveyard, a plaque, and a slab of concrete marking the location of the church's entrance.

Several pioneer-era homes flank old Peterson Road, now a shadow of its former self when stagecoaches and wagons rattled along it in a near-constant stream. Here and there, in the regenerated woods, foundation holes remind us of where settlers staked their futures.

The Uffington that was the thriving economic heart of Draper Township is gone. There can be no going back. History doesn't work that way. The best that we can do is remember the community and those who lived, loved, and lost there.

 To Get There

Uffington lies east of Highway 11. Follow Highway 118 east, turning south on Hawn Road (named, naturally, for the general store proprietor). The westernmost of Uffington's two centres huddled around the intersection of Hawn and Peterson Roads, two kilometres south. Head east along Peterson Road, watching for the renovated school and St. Paul's Anglican Cemetery. The balance of the village's remnants is strung out along Uffington Road (Muskoka Road 20), including the Orange Hall just to the south.

FALKENBURG JUNCTION

(Macauley Township, Muskoka District)

The land around Falkenburg Junction was unspectacular. The forests were just as thick and dark as elsewhere in Muskoka, the soil similarly threadbare, but the location did have one thing going for it: it was here that the Muskoka and Parry Sound Colonization Roads met. As the tides of settlement began to push newcomers into the northern reaches of Ontario, traffic along these colonization roads increased. As a result, the crossroads became a vital nexus through which commerce and settlers passed to points throughout the district. The formation of a community was inevitable. In fact, the village that emerged subsisted largely by catering to the needs of the road-weary.

Among Falkenburg Junction's first settlers was Thomas W. George, who arrived in 1860 as an eager 30-year-old to begin clearing a farm from the forest. Not content to remain a mere farmer, he erected a steam-powered shingle mill to provide roofing for homesteaders, as well as a store selling dry goods and provisions. As if that didn't keep him busy enough, George then established a crude log inn called the Junction Hotel. It didn't matter to him or his patrons that the whiskey served was manufactured with questionable ingredients in a backlot still, or that lacking a tavern licence, his entire establishment was illegal. The township council turned a blind eye to George's tavern and illegal distillery, so why should the residents be concerned? The seemingly tireless man even added a store to the rustic enterprise.

When George opened his businesses, there was hardly a community to speak of. Falkenburg Junction's population stood at only a couple of dozen people spread out over a handful of roadside farms. But every year more and more homesteaders arrived. Soon, the growing settlement merited a post office, with newly arrived William Holditch appointed as postmaster. Born in 1838, he left his Markham home around 1864 and headed for new prospects in Muskoka. There, he wrote himself into history for reasons beyond merely being Falkenburg Junction's inaugural postmaster: his marriage to Elizabeth Willson in 1866, officiated by his father-in-law, Gilman Willson, no less, was the first wedding in Bracebridge.

Arriving shortly on Holditch's heels was Matthias Moore, a man who did more than anyone to shape the destiny of Falkenburg Junction. And yet he was perhaps as unlikely a pioneer homesteader as one could find. Moore was a military man who had the makings of a distinguished career in the British Army. After being commissioned as a young officer in the prestigious Life Guards Regiment in 1845 and having the honour of riding in the 1852 funeral procession of Arthur Wellesley, the Duke of Wellington, Moore served bravely in the Crimean War of 1853–56. By 1864, he was due for promotion but instead was passed over for a younger, inexperienced officer whose wealthy family purchased the rank. Moore was naturally embittered. Turning his back on Britain, he headed for Canada.

Coming from wealth and comfort, Moore and his family were completely unprepared for the realities of life in the Canadian bush. Their first year was nearly disastrous. Upon arriving, Moore pitched a tent, naively believing it would be sufficient to shelter his family for the winter. When a neighbour asked when Moore intended to build a cabin, he replied that he had plenty of "good English blankets" to keep his family warm until spring. The neighbour smiled at the innocence of the English newcomer and rode off, returning a few days later with a crew who proceeded to erect a cabin for

The sawmill employed about a dozen men, all of whom were area farmers desperately in need of an additional source of income. Many more found winter employment cutting and hauling logs from the bush.

the Moores. One shudders to think about what hardships the family would have faced had not these more experienced settlers lent a hand.

Although his start was hardly encouraging, Moore would become the single most important figure in Falkenburg Junction's history. He owned most of the land directly adjacent to the crossroads and decided to subdivide it into two-tenth-hectare residential lots, allowing the community to grow and take on the true appearance of a village. Moore was confident that Falkenburg Junction would prosper and continue to develop, and for a time he was right. Continuous traffic along the roads did spur growth. Dozens of people were attracted to the bustling hamlet, which came to include David Galloway's shoe shop, John Jackson's smithy, and an Orange Lodge. By 1872, Moore was running the village post office. But by far the village's most lucrative enterprise was the sawmill Moore erected.

Construction of the sawmill commenced on November 11, 1872, a date Moore marked simply in his diary with the line, "cutting rafters and logs for mill." On November 16, the frame of the mill was raised. "Quite a sensation," wrote Moore. The mill was unique in that it incorporated some of the conventions of traditional water-powered mills and others of the more modern steam-powered variety. Because it was steam-driven, the mill was freed from the constraints of requiring a ready water source to run the machinery, and yet Moore painstakingly dug a millpond to serve it.

In the autumn, the water was drained from the pond by a pipe in the south end. Over the course of the winter, logs that had been felled from the surrounding forest were hauled by horses to the drained pond and dumped there. Prior to spring, the exit pipe was blocked and the pond filled naturally as the snow melted. Logs were floated in this artificial pond, and as was the case with a water-powered mill, were pulled up a chute by chains to the waiting blades when needed. It was a unique setup, one rarely seen, but it worked.

Despite having no previous milling experience, Matthias Moore was a man of ambition who threw himself into the role of lumberman with

Logging, an industry that sustained Falkenburg Junction for most of its history, began in 1872 when Matthias Moore built a sawmill. Despite having no experience, Moore threw himself into the role of lumberman. The mill outlived him. He died in 1893; the mill burned down in 1914.

unbridled enthusiasm. The sawmill employed about a dozen men, all of whom were area farmers struggling to cultivate crops in the thin soil and who therefore desperately needed an additional source of income.

Settling a new land was full of hardships and privations. Despite this, or perhaps because of it, the people of Falkenburg Junction never lost faith in God. As in almost every 19th-century pioneer community, it wasn't long after settling in that the people of Falkenburg Junction began to turn their thoughts to building a church. So a Methodist one, the first in Muskoka, was erected in 1863. A decade later, Anglicans started to think it was their turn. Matthias Moore was the driving force behind this movement. When he subdivided his land into lots, he made sure to set aside half a hectare upon which to build a church, and as one of the original church wardens, he was involved in organizing the congregation, raising funds for construction, and planning the church's design. Moore also provided lumber and shingles from his mill, and construction commenced in August 1875. Even though slowed by heavy rains, work was completed by October. St. George's

Education was a luxury few boys enjoyed much of, since they, like those pictured, were needed on farms and at the mill. Falkenburg Junction's School Section (SS) No. 3 Macauley opened in 1870, likely in a former settler's cabin; in 1887, it was replaced by a new building.

Anglican Church was officially consecrated and opened on February 6, 1875, with a ceremony conducted by the bishop of Algoma.

Every village of any size boasted its own schoolhouse, and Falkenburg Junction was no different. School Section (SS) No. 3 Macauley was built in 1870 and stood on the northern end of the community (Lot 4, Concession 11). No one knows what this school looked like; there are no written records and no photographs were taken of it. One assumes it was of log construction. In 1887, the school was replaced by a new building that served youth for more than half a century. In the school yard rested a massive erratic, a rock deposited by the retreating glaciers of the last ice age. Children delighted in climbing on it and playing King of the Castle.

Falkenburg Junction wasn't without drama. For the first decade of the village's existence, the only real crime was Thomas George's illicit distillery and unlicensed tavern. That changed suddenly one day in 1872, when the door to the post office burst open and a masked desperado stalked in. Levelling a pistol at the clerk — history doesn't record who was operating the post office that day — he demanded all the cash, money orders, and stamps. The valuables were handed over, and the bandit raced from the building, vaulting onto a waiting horse and beating a hasty retreat. No one was ever apprehended for the crime.

The robbery shattered the calm in Falkenburg Junction but didn't slow its growth. By mid-decade, the community was at the peak of its fortunes. In addition to the two hotels, sawmill, church, and school, it now boasted a blacksmith, an Orange Lodge, a shoemaker's shop, and three general stores. Although first on the scene, Thomas George wasn't around to witness the prosperity. By 1868, he had been put out of business by local officials for operating without a liquor licence, and in a pique of anger, stormed off to Parry Sound. The hotel was now operating under the new and completely legal proprietorship of William Brown, a plasterer by trade. Another establishment, the Wellington Hotel, was opened by Charles Percival. The two inns did steady business; there was enough to go around. It appeared as if Falkenburg Junction was stamped indelibly on the map.

But as quickly as prosperity had come, it was stolen away even faster. The culprit was the Northern and Pacific Junction Railway, later part of

Canadian National Railways. Incorporated in March 1881 to construct a line from Gravenhurst to Callander and eventually to Sault St. Marie, the railway inexplicably spurned Falkenburg Junction by running its tracks and building a station three kilometres to the south. When the tracks were opened in January 1886, it was the death knell for the community.

A new village called Falkenburg Station sprouted around the railway stop, and like a weed, sapped the vitality from Falkenburg Junction. Businesses from Falkenburg Junction began to relocate there, and soon the upstart was overshadowing its predecessor. Those shops that didn't migrate to the rail side slowly withered away from a drought of both business and hope. The Junction Hotel, for example, simply disappeared from records around 1888, by which time traffic along Muskoka Road had dwindled to a mere trickle. Presumably, it was just closed one day by the despairing owner. The inn's rival, the Wellington Hotel, had a more dramatic ending. In 1889, it was owned by J. Roscoe, the village blacksmith, and operated under the name Roscoe House. That April, a fire broke out at the blacksmith shop. Embers carried aloft by gusts of warm wind landed atop the hotel, and soon the building was aflame. Both businesses burned to the ground, as did a neighbouring barn.

St. George's Anglican Church didn't survive the arrival of the railway, either. In early November 1886, it was carefully dismantled and sledded down to Falkenburg Station, where it was rebuilt. Matthias Moore remained active. One of his final acts was overseeing the addition of a new chancel and vestry, built in 1890 using material from an unused log church in Bardsville. The Falkenburg Junction postal contract, which had been in the Moore name since 1872, was revoked on October 6, 1894, and a new post office opened at Falkenburg Station.

The railway was devastating for Falkenburg Junction, but a further blow was struck a few decades later when even the roads were diverted past the village, hastening its descent into a backwater. By the turn of the century, the population had dwindled from a high of about 250 to fewer than 40.

And yet, while the railway spelled doom for Falkenburg Junction, it brought increased prosperity for the Moore family. Trains meant easier access to distant markets and greater demand for lumber. When Matthias

Moore died of pneumonia in 1893, the mill was at the height of its profitability. Moore's widow, Susan, their sons, Arthur, Saxon, and Chad, and their grandson, George Bernard, carried on in his absence. It was familial strife more than any other factor that undermined the business.

When Susan died in 1910, she inexplicably deeded the property and its assets, including the sawmill, to Arthur alone. Understandably angered by this slight, Saxon and George Bernard refused to work at the mill (Chad was dead by then, killed in a hunting accident). Three years later, during what was an unusually hot and dry summer, a raging brush fire threatened the sawmill. Men, women, and children battled for several days to beat back the flames and preserve the vital industry. In the end, they were successful. The mill was saved, but the reprieve was only temporary. A fire originating in the boiler claimed the mill in November 1914.

That wasn't the end of milling in Falkenburg Junction, however. The slighted George Bernard had built a small sawmill of his own not far away. In 1917, three years after fire razed his grandfather's mill, he approached Arthur for permission to move operations to the old millpond. Arthur agreed for a monthly rent of $75.

In 1917, George Bernard Moore built a sawmill on the site of his grandfather's recently burned-out mill. He and his wife lived in the home (still standing) overlooking the mill atop Moore's Hill. The mill operated until 1932, when George Bernard moved his operation to Falkenburg Station.

George Bernard and his wife, Charlotte, lived in a home just north of the sawmill atop what became known as Moore Hill. Their five sons were born there. They also made room to board the schoolteachers employed at SS No. 3. "Nana enjoyed the company of these women, who perhaps offered a respite from the six male occupants of the house," recalled Patricia Moore Evans, the granddaughter of George Bernard and Charlotte. "These women shared their books with Nana — she was an insatiable reader — at a time when books were scarce. One young teacher, Marie Yeoman, ended up marrying their son, Lloyd."

A tragedy struck the family in 1931, inflicting a wound they never really recovered from. Aubrey Moore, known as Bob, was said to be the nicest and most popular of the four Moore boys. He was certainly Charlotte's favourite. Bob came home from playing hockey on the millpond with a severe headache and back pain. The condition became progressively more severe, and he was rushed to Toronto by train for treatment. He died of meningitis. "None of the family would ever talk about Uncle Bob's death and could rarely bring

In 1927, George Bernard Moore paid $9,500 for a Linn tractor to haul logs from the woods to feed his mills. It was a worthy investment. Not only could it pull seven sleighs of logs, but Moore also used it to power a planing mill in the summer and ploughed roads under contract with local municipalities. Discarded and left in the bush in 1953, the Linn tractor was later restored by the Muskoka Pioneer Power Association and is displayed at the annual Muskoka Pioneer Power Show.

themselves to even mention his name," explained Patricia. "Nana was devastated and never got over the loss. When she was old and showing the first signs of dementia, she began calling one of her grandsons 'Bob' and would carry on conversations with him, sometimes tearfully saying how much she had missed him. Heartbreaking."

George Bernard milled in Falkenburg Junction until 1932, when, to expand the business and perhaps escape the scene of the recent tragedy, he moved the family a kilometre and a half south to Falkenburg Station. There, he purchased the home and general store of E.W. Hay — which currently resides in the recreated pioneer village at Muskoka Heritage Place in Huntsville — and built a larger sawmill that endured for decades.

"My grandparents were polar opposites," said Patricia. "Grandpa was tall and dwarfed Grandma, who stood about five foot one and maybe weighed 105 pounds. He had a very commanding appearance. He had a loud voice,

In 1931, George Bernard Moore moved his family from Falkenburg Junction to Falkenburg Station, where he purchased the store founded by Edward Wheatley (E.W.) Hay in 1878. After Hay died in 1926, his widow, Emma, ran the business until selling out to Moore. The store continued to run under the Moores until 1953 and was later moved to Muskoka Heritage Place in Huntsville, where it forms part of a recreated pioneer village.

prone to yelling — it was probably a habit to be heard above the saws. And you think troopers can swear? You should hear saw millers!"

George Bernard had been hardened by years of tough labour and a childhood tragedy that saw him lose a mother and then be abandoned by a grieving father. But while intimidating, George was a gentle soul, and Patricia loved him deeply.

George Bernard and Charlotte Moore were polar opposites. He was tall with a commanding appearance, prone to swearing and yelling — habits probably born in the noisy sawmill — and full of life. She, by contrast, was tiny, barely over 1.5 metres, never sang or laughed, never smiled, and was extremely quiet. They were nonetheless devoted to each other and true partners in raising a family, operating the milling business, and later, the general store.

Charlotte, by contrast, was quiet, almost reserved. Her legs showed signs of early childhood malnutrition, almost impossibly thin, but Patricia recalls she had beautiful reddish-brown hair that was so long to young eyes that it seemed as if it had never been cut. "I never heard my grandmother laugh," Patricia told me. "She didn't smile or sing. She worked."

George Bernard and Charlotte were an unlikely couple, but together they carried on the Moore lumbering legacy, eventually passing it on to a fourth generation. But that was in Falkenburg Station. After the Moores left Falkenburg Junction, the few remaining families followed suit. In 1938, the one-room school graduated its final, tiny class. It represented the last vestige of Falkenburg Junction. The school's closure drew a curtain on the short-lived village, which had finally run its course.

Today, the ruined remnant of the Moore mill serves as the ghostliest relic of Falkenburg Junction's past. It lies on private property behind the weed-choked millpond, partially hidden by regenerated forest. Overlooking the mill is Moore's Hill, topped by the home of George Bernard and his wife, Charlotte, built in 1903 and expanded in 1920. St. George's Anglican Church is gone from the community (closed since 2018, though still standing), but the pioneer Moore Cemetery remains. Only a handful of forlorn headstones occupy the grounds, pitifully few for a village that lasted nearly half a century. Almost certainly there are many more graves whose markers have rotted away or sunk into the ground. Among those headstones remaining are ones belonging to members of the Holditch and Moore families.

A bow can't be tied on the Falkenburg Junction story without mentioning the fate of the Moores and their mill. The family tradition of milling came to a sudden end on the night of May 14, 1960, when a fire broke out and consumed the mill, several outbuildings, and a vast quantity of manufactured lumber in a storage shed.

"It was a devastating loss, not only for the Moore family but all those who were employed there, some of whom had been working for the family for generations," said Patricia Moore Evans, noting there was little insurance coverage on the mill.

The Moores, who had milled since 1871, would mill no more.

To Get There

Drive north from Bracebridge along Muskoka Road 4 to Falkenburg Station, and on the right, you will see St. George's Anglican Church. Then continue north. After crossing the railway tracks, turn right onto Moore Road. The T-intersection ahead was where Muskoka Road and Parry Sound Colonization Road met — the heart of Falkenburg Junction. Thomas George's Junction Hotel stood on the southwest corner. To the south lies the cemetery, the one-time home of George Bernard and Charlotte Moore, and the sawmill. North of the intersection stood the Wellington Hotel and Roscoe's blacksmith shop, the school, and the Orange Hall, all long gone.

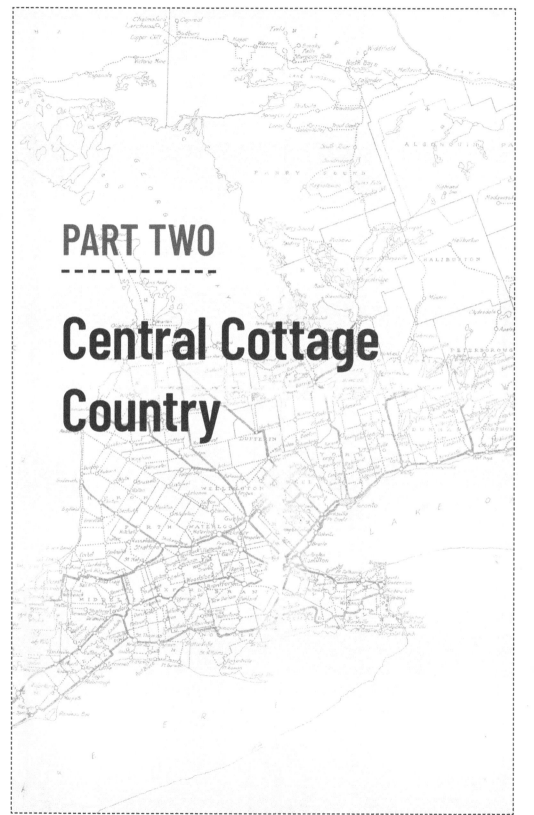

PART TWO

Central Cottage Country

SWORDS

(Seguin Township, Parry Sound District)

The former hamlet of Swords is wrapped in a ghostly shroud. There are unmistakable hints that life once flourished here, that a community had previously huddled around this railway crossing. And yet the weathered one-time general store and overgrown farm fields make it plain that time has passed this village by. Instead of the hum of sawmill blades echoing up from Maple Lake and the rumble of stagecoaches passing by, only deathly silence is heard. Swords is a ghost town — of that there's no doubt.

The lands bordering modern-day Tally Ho-Swords Road were initially settled by hardy settlers in the early 1870s — men and women who eagerly staked claim to lots and began to clear the bush to establish farms. Among them were members of the Sword clan: Thomas and Eliza and sons John, David, and Tom Junior. The story of Swords would be intertwined with this family. True, many others contributed to the tapestry of everyday life within the rural hamlet, but none had their fingers in as many pies as did the varied members of the Sword family. Their personal successes were reflected in those of the community.

Such contributions were in the future, however, because for decades after the Swords and their families arrived, there was no real municipality to speak of. All that existed was a collection of crude farmsteads spread over kilometres of dense forest. Many settlers would have found the forests daunting. Not so Scotland-born Thomas Sword. He was a career logging foreman, one of the best, and his services were in demand by logging companies across the region and beyond. It was never his intention to make his living primarily as a farmer, and he likely wasn't overly concerned with the lack of "civilization."

Farmsteads would very likely never have developed into a community of any real note if not for the vision and stubborn determination of one man — John Rudolphus Booth. He was a lumber and railway magnate whose holdings included the Canada Atlantic Railway, which stretched from Ottawa to the Maritimes. In the 1880s, he added extensive timber rights in Algonquin Park to his empire, and at that point, his thoughts turned to a railway line that would stretch across the Central Ontario Highlands. Its purpose would be twofold: to serve his immense new timber rights and by finishing the railway on the shores of Georgian Bay, share in the lucrative business of transporting Prairie grain eastward.

In July 1891, the Ottawa, Arnprior, and Parry Sound Railway (OA&PSR) was formed. Four years later, the line was complete, running from Ottawa in the east to Parry Sound in the west, and just by happenstance, it passed through Swords. This twist of fate, a surveyor's whim, assured Swords a bright, if brief, future. Except, of course, the hamlet wasn't called Swords then. When the railway established a flag stop there, it dubbed the building Maple Lake Station after the nearby body of water. Consequently, the community took the name as its own.

Booth's railway transformed the lives of the area settlers seemingly overnight, providing prosperity heretofore unimaginable by allowing the Maple Lake district to be opened to lumber interests. In 1894, the Ludgate Lumber Company, of which David Sword was a partner, purchased significant tracts of land and raised a large steam-powered sawmill on the shore of Maple Lake. Soon the woods rang with the sound of axes cutting into trees and the near-constant buzz of the sawmill echoing across the lake's placid surface.

Logging camps dotted the woods around Maple Lake, offering winter employment for local men. This camp was likely run by the Ludgate Lumber Company to provide logs for its mill on Maple Lake.

In winter, the frozen lake provided the easiest means of hauling logs to the mill, far simpler than over the rolling terrain and through thick woods. On a good day, one could see up to 30 teams of horses moving logs across Maple Lake, some from as far away as 30 kilometres. During the summer, logs were floated across the lake by a device known as a horse crib — a huge raft of squared timbers with a spool just over a metre in diameter in the centre. Two-and-a-half-metre arms extended from the spool, to which a horse was hitched. Behind the crib was a block of as many as 2,000 logs. Men in a rowboat went a half kilometre ahead of the crib and dropped a 180-kilogram anchor. A sturdy rope ran from the anchor to the crib, and when the horse walked around the spool, the rope was slowly wound in, thereby towing the crib and the attached logs across the lake. Finished lumber, up to 12 cubic metres per day, was transported from the lakeshore to the railway siding a kilometre and a half distant by wagon, then trains shipped the lumber to market.

To facilitate its operations, the Ludgate Lumber Company built a string of homes for those workers who weren't local. The firm also built a

The rolling landscape around Swords was a challenge for logging company teamsters. It was far easier to haul logs across the frozen expanse of Maple Lake. Care had to be taken, though, since more than one heavily loaded sled fell through the ice.

false-fronted general store to cater to its employees. Wages were paid partly in tokens that could be redeemed for goods at the shop. On June 1, 1897, a post office opened in the store. Both the shop and post office were operated by managers employed by the lumber company.

In 1900, the Ludgate Lumber Company sold off its cabins and store. The mill was still thriving, so the decision was a curious one. Perhaps the ownership simply considered its operation a distraction. In any event, the shop was bought by 18-year-old Thomas Sword — though almost certainly his father, David, provided the money for the purchase — and continued to prosper. Thomas and his wife, Eliza, had six children in relatively rapid succession, making their quarters above the store increasingly uncomfortable. To address that, around 1919, Thomas built an addition on the north side of the building that served as a shop and post office. At the same time, the false facade and porch were removed from the original structure, which thereafter was solely used as the family residence.

In this early photo of Swords, circa 1900, we see the general store in the background at right and one of the homes built for sawmill workers at left. In the foreground are piles of tannin-rich hemlock bark ("tanbark") destined for tanning leather at either the William Taylor & Sons Tannery in Parry Sound or the Anglo Canadian Leather Company in Huntsville. Harvesting tanbark provided landowners with valuable income.

Thomas wasn't the only Sword to profit by the railway. Brother John and his wife, Annie, decided to build a hotel across from the general store and adjacent to the railway station, ensuring he could profit from local loggers as well as from those travelling by rail and road. The Maple Lake Hotel was a two-storey frame structure with a wide, shaded veranda, a dozen guest rooms offering comfortable, though certainly not lavish, accommodations, and a large bar. It was hardly stylish by the definition of the summer resorts then doing brisk business along the lakeshores in nearby Muskoka, but the hotel was considered the height of refinement in Christie Township.

At first, the hotel's main business came from serving drinks to the men working the logging camps in the area and labouring at the sawmill on the shore of nearby Maple Lake. Because the Maple Lake Hotel served as a watering hole for the loggers and mill hands, the barroom could become boisterous at times. It was the indomitable Annie Sword who kept the

The Maple Lake Hotel, built by John and Annie Sword, was frequented by summer tourists seeking a taste of the Canadian bush and by mill hands who descended on its barroom. The hotel thrived for a few decades before fading. Nothing but photos remain today.

booze-soaked men in line. Anyone who didn't meet her standards of behaviour was promptly ushered to the door.

Soon, the Maple Lake Hotel began to diversify its clientele. Summer tourists started to discover the location, especially Americans wishing to sample a taste of the "true northern wilds." With a clientele consisting of equal measures rough-and-tumble lumbermen and well-to-do vacationers, John and Annie had to make special considerations. "The bar had a separate entrance so that people wouldn't have to enter through the hotel," recalled Jack Sword, John and Annie's grand-nephew, who I interviewed in 2005. "You wouldn't want dirty mill hands trekking through the foyer, after all. Annie was also very strict about people being on their best behaviour, and they were always told to leave before they got too liquored up. She was a very proper, very formidable woman."

In addition to the hotel, John Sword also owned the Tally Ho Coach Line, which ran stages from the steamer docks at Rosseau and Port Cockburn to his hotel and beyond. To facilitate this business, he had a private phone line run

In addition to the Maple Lake Hotel, John Sword operated the Tally Ho Coach Line, which ran stages from the steamer docks at Rosseau and Port Cockburn to his hotel and beyond. To facilitate this business, he had a private phone line run from the hotel to those ports — the first anywhere in Christie Township.

from the hotel to those ports, enabling him to keep abreast of the comings and goings of steamships. That was the first phone line in Christie Township, predating public ones by more than a decade. John and Annie prospered and were considered the wealthiest people in the young hamlet of Maple Lake.

By the turn of the 20th century, Maple Lake Station had grown large enough that a clear need for a school to educate local children had emerged. To address this concern, James Smith donated a parcel of land on the east side of Swords Road about a kilometre south of the rail crossing, while money for the school's construction was loaned by Margaret Sword Waugh. The one-room School Section (SS) No. 1 was built in 1904. A stove stood in the centre of the room in a vain attempt to adequately warm the entire building. Shelves containing library books covered the lower half of the south wall, above which hung maps and charts. The school proudly boasted a piano, a luxury for that time.

The school also doubled as a community hall, and since there was no dedicated church in Swords, as a place of worship tended by a Methodist

The one-room Maple Lake/Swords school was opened in 1904. The village's youth were educated there until 1958; today it survives as a community centre.

minister from Orrville. Because nearly everyone would be arriving by wagon or sleigh, a drive shed was erected at the time of construction. This building, which was large enough to easily accommodate more than a dozen horses, stood at the southeast corner of the lot.

To cater to the growing community, the OA&PSR expanded its railway station at Maple Lake, though it was only ever a flag depot, meaning that trains stopped only when they were alerted that passengers or cargo awaited pickup. A larger wood-frame building, measuring about three and a half by seven metres, replaced the earlier and tinier station. Inside, there was a stove to provide warmth, benches for waiting passengers, and little else. A siding was built to facilitate the transfer of lumber cut at the nearby mill onto flatbeds, and there was a small freight shed where train crews left parcels or mail destined for the village.

Around 1914, John and Annie Sword decided to retire and sold the hotel to their nephew, Percival (Percy) Sword, and his new wife, Katherine. Their son, Jack, was born in the hotel in 1917 and spent the first eight years of his life running along its carpeted hallways and playing in its cavernous barroom. "It was a marvellous building and rather posh in its day," Jack remembered. "The bar was a large room, with mirrors hanging over the bars like you see in westerns. It had many modern features for the time. Copper funnels were used in those days to pipe alcohol from barrels to bottles. The building was also entirely lit by carbide gas, a rarity. Gas would be piped from storage tanks to the rooms, creating open flames in wall-mounted lamps. Not many buildings had carbide gas because it was expensive and very dangerous. Fires and even explosions could occur, but the hotel never once had a fire."

Change was underway at the store across the road, as well. After Thomas Sword died in 1921, the business was assumed by his widow, Lyde. She proved to be a capable businesswoman in her own right, managing both the store and its post office. During her time as postmaster, in 1925, the community learned that it would have to change its name because of confusion with another Maple Lake Station. In recognition of the family's role in shaping the village, residents unanimously voted to adopt the name Swords, and Lyde made it so officially.

This photo of Maple Lake Station, with the general store looking over its shoulder, can be dated to between 1919, when Thomas Sword built the one-storey addition to his shop, and 1925, when the community's name was changed from Maple Lake to Swords.

Five years later, a newly remarried Lyde sold the store to John Lawson and his son, Wilson. It was the younger Wilson and his wife, Harriet, who served as storekeepers. Neither had any previous experience running a business. Nonetheless, the couple proved successful at the new venture and guided the store for four decades.

By this time, a slow decline in the community's fortunes had already begun. With timber largely played out, the mill, which had been sold to the Shephard Lumber Company, closed, and families that were dependent on logging left in search of greener pastures. Furthermore, the very year the name of the community was changed from Maple Lake to Swords, the Maple Lake Hotel, the symbol of Sword status in the community, closed its doors.

But all wasn't lost, because the Ludgate/Shephard mill wasn't the only one to operate in Swords. Around the time this operation was winding down, local landowners John Lawson and his son, Wilson, started a mill of their own a few kilometres south of Swords where Sunny Shore Road and Tally Ho-Swords Road meet. This sawmill was much smaller, cutting lumber mostly for local consumption, but it was productive enough that the bush camp employed as many as two dozen men during the winter. The income was welcomed by local men, especially during the lean years of the Great Depression.

As evidence of the village's decline, its school was closed in December 1936 due to low attendance, and pupils were transported by wagon or sleigh to SS No. 2 in Edgington. In 1941, the Swords school reopened. The school population swelled when the Turtle Lake schoolhouse (SS No. 5) was shut in 1948 and its students were transferred to Swords. The Swords school remained in use for another decade before closing for good in 1958.

The general store provided welcome continuity in a village undergoing rapid change. Wilson and Harriet became as much a symbol of the community as the store itself. Their granddaughter, a very young Donna Haslehurst, spent summers with the couple. Even after the passage of 60 years, she has vivid memories of the store.

There was a long wooden counter across the back of the store beneath which were metal bins for dry goods such as flour. Each bin had a scoop in it, and above the bins, suspended from the ceiling, was a row of paper bags, different sizes to be chosen according to the amount of the order. Between the bins and bags on the counter was a scale where Harriet weighed flour, sugar, or salt.

"I was also fascinated by the ornate metal cash register," reminisces Donna. "Occasionally, to my great delight, my grandmother would allow me to hit the NO SALE button to hear the little bell ring and the drawer fly open. Also on the counter was a glass case, which opened from the back, so that my grandmother could reach in and extract the desired item. This case held candy, and we were strictly forbidden to touch it."

Behind the counter, the wall was covered with shelving where an assortment of canned and packaged goods was displayed for sale. "An old wooden telephone was still attached to that back wall," Donna remembers, "the kind that you had to wind up, pick up the earpiece, hold to your ear, and talk into the receiver on the wall. By the time I arrived on the scene, this wasn't in use anymore, and we were allowed to play with it. It was magical."

Donna explains further: "My grandfather worked at the John Lawson and Sons sawmill, so my grandmother ran the post office and store. When we were visiting, which we did for weeks at a time, the bell would ring in the store and my grandmother would go through the door from the kitchen into the store and close the door behind her. We were under strict instructions to remain quiet while there were customers in the store."

The community the Wilsons served slowly withered away as farms failed, the lumber industry dried up, and trains stopped passing through. Wilson and Harriet ran the store for almost 40 years despite an increasingly reduced clientele. The end came on January 31, 1967, when the post office was shut down upon the introduction of rural mail delivery in the area, and Harriet reluctantly turned the sign on the door to CLOSED permanently.

Over the decades since, the mists of time slowly but inevitably began to envelop Swords. No evidence remains of the hotel that once served loggers and American tourists in equal measure. It was torn down decades ago. No one has any idea where the railway station ended up; it was removed shortly after its closure in 1946. Two of the cabins built for mill employees stood until recently. Leaning precariously, rotting, spiderwebs the size of dinner platters hanging like curtains from door frames, they served as atmospheric

The one-time general store, battered and ramshackle, still stands alongside the rail crossing in Swords.

photo opportunities. They're gone, too. The Lawson mill site was flooded by beavers, eliminating any evidence that might have remained, and the site of the Ludgate/Shephard mill has now been swallowed by the forest.

And yet just enough remains to remind us of Swords's past. The general store, faded advertisements still clinging to the walls, looks out onto a new century through cracked windows. The porch sags, the paint peels, the roof leaks, and yet the store still stands. On again/off again renovations are underway to preserve it. One can only hope the endeavour is successful, since the general store has character in spades.

Beside the store is the OA&PSR line. Although the tracks have long since been lifted, the roadbed, bisecting Swords Road and disappearing into the forest on either side, remains in excellent shape as the Seguin Recreational Trail, used in all seasons by hikers, ATV riders, and snowmobilers. Walk east, and after 10 minutes or so, you'll come to where the tracks crossed a ravine. The abutments, though small in scale compared to many along the line, provide a sense of the challenges faced when John Rodolphus Booth embarked on building his railway across this rugged landscape.

The schoolhouse, just a short distance to the south, is perhaps the most enduring symbol of Swords's past, and most notably, its character. After the school closed, the township agreed to sell the building to the Maple Lake Club for $1. It has been in continuous use as a community centre, sustained largely by funds raised during an annual summer pie social and charity auction. The school remains largely unchanged from the time when its bell summoned children to class. Even the hand-powered pump that students drew their drinking water from is still there. The most notable difference, save for the absence of the sounds of children at play or reciting lessons, is the drive shed, which has long since been torn down.

Donna Haslehurst continues to visit Swords from time to time whenever the urge for nostalgic reflection compels her. When she looks at the store, she doesn't see a weathered derelict. Instead, she only imagines the vibrant store of yesterday and the warm faces of her beloved grandparents. And when she pictures the school, she's reminded of sitting under the pine trees with a doll while her grandmother was busy inside, or the magical memory of attending a Christmas concert back when it still hosted classes.

"Swords was a place and a community that defies description in modern terms," she tells me. "It wasn't perfect, but it was genuine."

 To Get There

To reach Swords, take Highway 518 west from Highway 400, just south of Parry Sound. Turn south on Tally Ho-Swords Road and drive about four kilometres south to the railway crossing and the general store. The school is on the west, slightly farther on. Immerse yourself in area history by driving south to Highway 141, then turn west. About a kilometre later stop in at the Humphrey Museum, a converted one-room log schoolhouse dating to circa 1878. The exhibits and artifacts help paint a picture of the region's development.

6

SEGUIN FALLS

(Seguin Township, Parry Sound District)

Erily silent, the battered ruins and empty lots of Seguin Falls are testimony to the hardships and disillusionment faced by the hardy settlers who founded this community. A crossroads hamlet — and a busy one at that — Seguin Falls was established on the Nipissing Colonization Road where it intersected with Christie Road. One of 25 colonization roads in the government's effort to open the Canadian Shield to farming, Nipissing Road was cut through the dense bush from Lake Rosseau in the south to Lake Nipissing in the north. Although much of the land was rock and swamp, little villages developed along its length, most of them centred around an inn that provided rest and comfort for tired stagecoach travellers.

Seguin Falls began as one such stopping place. It originated in 1865, when 42-year-old David Francis Burk arrived and built a roadside hotel with attached post office. He was so certain of a bright future that he turned his back on a prosperous life in Oshawa on Lake Ontario that included a comfortable farm and a stint as town reeve. Burk was no stranger to the hospitality industry, having grown up around his family's hotel in Oshawa, and it showed as his Seguin Falls enterprise gained a wide reputation for hospitality. "The traveller will find an excellent temperance hotel at Seguin Falls, the proprietor of which, Mr. D.F. Burk, is a most genial and hospitable host," declared the *Guide Book & Atlas of Muskoka and Parry Sound Districts* for 1879. Referring to Burk's wife, Henrietta, the writer went on to add, "Nor should we forget to praise the excellent cuisine of his good lady." Sadly, Burk died the same year this endorsement was written, leaving his wife to continue without him.

But, of course, Seguin Falls was more than just its hotel. As with all strategic crossroads, a lively little village emerged at the busy junction. Burk, who owned all four corners of the crossroads, donated land for a log school before he died. The Beasley gristmill ground grain into flour for bread, churches were devoted to Methodist and Anglican denominations, and Adam Fitzer served as village blacksmith. Fitzer must have been tireless; in addition to pounding metal into shape over a glowing hearth, he also ran a boarding house and store and served as postmaster from 1883 to 1886. The Guelph Lumber Company, which owned several hundred hectares of land in the vicinity, operated a sawmill. Numerous farmsteads strung out along either road of the crossroads brought the population to well above 100.

Burk's widow elected not to manage the Seguin Falls Hotel on her own for very long. Instead, she recruited Henry and Emma Pletzer to operate it on her behalf for several years. The couple had come north from Blyth, Ontario, in search of new hope and possibilities. After disembarking from a steamship at Rosseau, they trudged up Nipissing Road. Seguin Falls wasn't their intended destination; they had planned to go farther north. Family lore says they intended to head for New Liskeard, though that clearly couldn't have been the case, since the first settlers didn't put down roots there for almost three more decades. But because the only conveyance they could secure was an open buggy, as opposed to a more sheltering covered wagon, they grew weary of the hardship. When offered the job of running the hotel, they eagerly agreed and put a halt to their migration north, at least for the time being. Later, they helped found the Parry Sound hamlet of Orange Valley.

Eventually, Henrietta Burk sold the Seguin Falls Hotel to William E. Fleming, who updated the facilities and advertised the place as having "good, clean, comfortable rooms, a tidy dining room and a well-furnished table." Clientele was a blend of travellers seeking overnight accommodations and loggers revelling in the barroom. Thankfully, Fleming had little trouble keeping rough-and-ready lumberjacks in line, since he stood a towering 1.9 metres tall. He also put his imposing size to good use in one of the most infamous events to take place in the village's history.

On June 11, 1896, two men were spotted walking through Seguin Falls toward Parry Sound. One, a tall fellow with a straggly black beard, was James Mullen. The other was "a tough-looking character, a foreigner speaking poor English," the Swede Christian Hanson. Mullen was a manual labourer from Allenwood, near Elmvale, in Simcoe County. He frequently had to kiss his wife and their 11 children goodbye and set off in search of work. In this case, he was hoping to find employment with the Ottawa, Arnprior, and Parry Sound Railway (OA&PSR), then just being completed into Parry Sound. Failing that, he hoped to hire on with a sawmill or even

Lumber baron J.R. Booth's Ottawa, Arnprior, and Parry Sound Railway (OA&PSR) was the longest privately owned railway in the world. Its arrival shaped Seguin Falls. The original crossroads settlement picked up and moved trackside to hitch its fortunes to the railway. Seguin Falls thrived as a shipping depot for lumber and farm goods.

spend the winter felling trees in a deep-woods logging camp. Mullen had gone as far as Emsdale by train and then headed on foot for Parry Sound. Somewhere along the way, he was joined by Hanson, also looking for employment. Seeking companionship, the pair walked together.

Evening saw Mullen and Hanson arrive at Seguin Falls. Hoping for an inexpensive bed for the night, they approached Christina Fry's boarding house but were turned away. Instead, they decided to bed down in the hayloft of a barn located just south of the crossroads, opposite the school. An exhausted Mullen fell into a deep sleep. Hanson, however, had more insidious things than sleep on his mind. Using Mullen's own walking stick, he smashed in the left side of his face, killing him. He then stripped the body, stashed it below the threshing floor, and made off into the dark with all the victim's belongings.

Three days later, Mullen's body was discovered by schoolchildren. A hue and cry went up, and Constable Good was summoned. Because numerous people had seen Mullen and Hanson together, the lawman had a suspect. Since he also knew what direction the two had been headed, Good also had an idea where to hunt for his suspect. Constable Good recruited William Fleming, an upstanding citizen and a brave, imposing figure, as deputy and raced off toward Parry Sound.

Hanson was found at Rose Point with incriminating evidence in his possession, including the bloodstained walking stick. Outnumbered and cowed by the towering Fleming, he meekly succumbed. Good and Fleming returned to Seguin Falls with their prisoner in tow and locked him up for the night at the Seguin Falls Hotel. The next day, Hanson was dispatched to Parry Sound, where a trial, guilty verdict, and life incarceration awaited him.

The village faced a crossroads of its own when, in 1897, lumber baron John Adolphus Booth pushed his OA&PSR across the highlands of Ontario. Villagers were dismayed to learn that the tracks would cross Nipissing Road several kilometres south of Seguin Falls. But instead of allowing disillusionment to drive them away from their community, the residents simply moved the six-kilometre distance and built a new Seguin Falls alongside the tracks. In the end, the railway was a blessing, bringing renewed prosperity to a village that was already stagnating as farmers recognized the futility of raising crops in the barren soil.

Whereas the first Seguin Falls was a crossroads hamlet and farming community, the new one was a lumbering centre pure and simple. The great forests produced a rich yield of timber that until the arrival of the railway couldn't be fully exploited. Logs by the hundred were shipped out aboard labouring trains, while every spring, a tidal wave of timber was shepherded down the Seguin River to the massive mills and steamer docks at Parry Sound. In addition, many logs were cut locally at a large trackside sawmill belonging to the Spence Lumber Company. Countless railcars piled high with lumber were sent to Parry Sound, where the lumber was loaded aboard vessels bound for distant markets.

Starved of business, the Seguin Falls Hotel closed. Replacing it, in Seguin Falls, was the King George Hotel. Built around 1908 for 23-year-old Thomas McKinnon, it was an impressive structure that sat near the roadway and tracks. Although some travellers sought respite here, the hotel served primarily as a bunkhouse and watering hole for those engaged in the timber industry. According to veteran lumberman Guy Smith, the King George was

This view from the turn of the 20th century reveals the size of then-flourishing Seguin Falls, home to a hotel and store, half a dozen other businesses, two churches, a school, a community hall, and a railway station and siding.

"a pretty rough place ... the river drivers would go in there and have quite a howdy-do." In addition to serving drinks to rugged bushmen and providing a place to sleep off their hangovers when the revelry had run its course, the hotel also housed a well-stocked general store.

Thomas McKinnon enjoyed considerable success as a businessman, but his life wasn't entirely blessed. In 1923, he endured a tragedy so painful that it was said to haunt him for the remainder of his days. In 1919, Thomas's sister, 22-year-old Pearl Victoria, wed John Stevenson, a soldier recently returned from service in the First World War. There were problems in the marriage almost from the start. John had a fiery temper — today, he might have been diagnosed with post-traumatic stress disorder — and he seemed to have trouble finding gainful employment. By 1923, the couple and their two young children were forced to move in with Pearl and Thomas's mother, Mary Jane (their father, Angus, had died six years prior). Relations between Mary Jane and John were strained and came to a head on October 22, when a heated argument led to Mary Jane kicking the man out of her home.

John was livid, boiling with rage. He returned to the house a short while later, burst through the door, levelled a pistol at Mary Jane, and fired. She was killed instantly. Next, he turned the weapon on Pearl and discharged two shots into her, then fled.

Neighbours heard the gunfire and rushed to the scene. They found two-year-old Allan Albert wailing, while infant Emily was clutched tightly in the arms of her badly wounded mother. Pearl was raced by train to hospital and lingered for a time, but her wounds were too grievous, and she slipped away a few days later. John was arrested, tried, and convicted of double homicide. Thomas McKinnon likely found little comfort in the verdict but soldiered on as well as one could in such painful circumstances and served as a pillar in the community.

Seguin Falls was at its peak at the time of these twin tragedies, home to half a dozen other businesses, Methodist and Anglican churches, a community hall, a fine brick school built in 1922, and a railway station with a small stockyard for farmers shipping cattle to market. A row of simple cabins occupied by mill workers perched on the rocky outcrops north of the

Shopping was done at one of several stores that operated in Seguin Falls over the years. The Vigrass store was founded by Percy Vigrass but was run for much of its existence by Howard Vigrass, Percy's nephew, and his wife, Orma. It closed in the early 1940s after the store lost its post office contract.

railway tracks, while larger, more stately homes lay along the community's only street south of the tracks.

Shopping was predominantly done at the false-fronted Vigrass general store, which also housed the village post office. Founded by Percy Vigrass, the business was taken over by his nephew Howard Vigrass and his wife, Orma, around 1929. Howard, part of an extended family that was well respected in the vicinity, was a product of Nipissing Road, having been born just a few kilometres north of Seguin Falls at Dufferin Bridge in 1901. Orma hailed from farther south in Simcoe County, but with her energy and warm personality fitted in quickly. The couple and their store became linchpins of the community.

"I remember Howard and Orma and their store well," recalls Merv Brown, who attended school in Seguin Falls for a few years in the 1930s. "As a young lad at the time, what sticks out most in my memory are the jars of hard candy lined up on the counter. Howard would let me take one for free. It was a big decision and required some time."

Until the late 1920s, the railway tracks through Seguin Falls rumbled and vibrated day and night as a constant stream of trains, as many as 20 every 24 hours, chugged through the village. Then, in 1933, an ice floe destroyed a bridge on the line in Algonquin Park. Canadian National Railways (CNR) elected not to undertake the costly rebuild and through service stopped. The rails now ended at Scotia Junction and the CNR's Toronto–North Bay line. After that, the number of trains passing through Seguin Falls dwindled to a mere handful per day, and the village lost its importance as a whistle stop.

However, other factors had already been at work undermining the community. By the 1930s, lumbering as a major industry had ended in the area. This struck a serious blow to farmers, who derived their main source of income from winter logging. Their farms could provide what was required to feed their families and little more. With no recourse, farmers began fleeing their rocky land, abandoning farms that in many cases had taken two generations to establish.

Another blow came a decade later, in 1941, when Howard and Orma Vigrass lost their post office licence. Sweet-toothed Merv Brown and indeed the entire community were saddened when the store closed shortly thereafter. For shopping (and candy), people had to look elsewhere. Thankfully, they didn't have to venture far.

By the 1940s, traffic along Nipissing Road had dropped to almost nothing, while logging in the region was much reduced. There was no longer any business to keep the King Edward Hotel open. Instead, Thomas and Mary Jane McKinnon pivoted and turned the building into a general store.

Deborah Patterson, raised in Parry Sound but summering in Seguin Falls with her grandparents, has fond childhood memories of the store. "I spent many a day in the former hotel," she says wistfully. "I always went in for a pop and a long red licorice. I would go back and help Mrs. McKinnon with odd chores. She was such a nice lady."

Seguin Falls by this time was greatly reduced in size if not spirit. The community hall still regularly rang to the sound of square dances that attracted family and friends from neighbouring communities. Feet stomped on wooden floors, a lively band played, and voices sang gaily along. The dances took on particular importance during the dark days of the Second World War when there were empty places around almost every dinner table and worries for husbands, sons, brothers, and fathers fighting on distant battlefields.

Merv Brown's family was musically inclined and were often asked to come down from Spence to play at these dances. "I vividly remember that at the end of these dances everyone would gather at the front of the raised platform where the orchestra sat. Mom would play the pump organ and they would sing war tunes like 'It's a Long Way to Tipperary,' 'When Johnny Comes Marching Home,' and so forth," he says. "Tom and Mrs. McKinnon loved to sing — Tom, with his big belly, would shout out the words to these songs. These dances raised spirits for people on the home front and money to support those overseas."

In 1955, after the railway completely ceased operation, the final general store shut its doors, the post office was only two years away from being closed, and the population of the village had shrunk from 480 in 1921 to

Thomas Vickers came with his parents from England to settle in Rock Hill, a village in Parry Sound District that, like Seguin Falls, became a ghost town. Later, the family moved to Nipissing Road, where Thomas wed Charlotte Watkinson. Together, they opened the Empire Store in Seguin Falls.

fewer than 50. Within a decade, almost all the homes stood vacant except perhaps as seasonal residences.

The landmark King Edward Hotel stood empty for decades thereafter, overlooking silent roads in the community it had once served. In 1988, the building burned to the ground, leaving only foundations and the stone fireplace and chimney as markers of its existence.

Several newer homes have been built on pioneer-era plots, but nonetheless some remnants remain, most notably the former school, now a cottage. Although heavily renovated, the Vigrass house is still there, as well. Farther on is the former railway bed, now called the Seguin Recreational Trail, used by hikers in the summer and snowmobilers once snow shrouds the landscape. South from Highway 518 on the old Nipissing Road the former stagecoach highway becomes a narrow trail lined by tall grass, weeds, and regrown forest. Eventually, it becomes impassable to anything save for all-terrain vehicles. Lurking among the foliage here are several of the village's former homes and farmsteads, all of them abandoned and in varying stages of decay.

The Vickers family's homestead was just north of Seguin Falls. It and many others like it remained standing, though in a ruined state, until recent decades. Little wonder Nipissing Road gained the moniker "Road of Broken Dreams."

The only sound to cut through the funeral-like hush is the howl of wind through the pines. Here, at Seguin Falls, where the shrill whistle of steam engines once cut through the air, where the roar of the sawmill seldom stopped, deathly silence reigns supreme.

 To Get There

From Highway 400, head east on Highway 518. Thirty kilometres later, you'll reach Nipissing Road. North, you'll wind your way through a string of one-time farming hamlets — North Seguin, Dufferin Bridge, and Spence — before reaching Magnetawan. But for our purposes, we'll want to turn south on Nipissing Road to find the remnants of Seguin Falls.

WHITEHALL

(Township of McMurrich Monteith, Parry Sound District)

Right up until the day he died in 1981, Edgar White remembered with unusual clarity his childhood growing up in the rural community of Whitehall, named, he proudly reminded everyone, for his family. He took great pleasure regaling listeners with stories of bygone days and the hard but fulfilling life people led there.

Edgar lived the back half of his life in South River near Algonquin Park, but the members of his family said he never really left Whitehall, where he was born and which his family helped found in the heady days of Parry Sound settlement in the late 19th century. His heart still belonged there, rooted to it by family connections and a deep love of the forests and lakes he grew up surrounded by. Whitehall was a hamlet but loomed large in Edgar's memories and that of others who at one time called the place home.

Whitehall honours Edgar's family, but the Whites weren't the first to plunge into the dense forests to settle this corner of McMurrich Township.

Two families, the Rolfes and Smiths, arrived in the Whitehall area years before the Whites appeared. Neither, however, left a distinctive or enduring mark on the region.

William and Louisa Rolfe, the first to homestead in the region, were both born in England but met and married in Hamilton, Ontario, in 1877. A year later, they were in McMurrich Township, where a son, John William, was born. William and Louisa initially had 120 hectares and later added another 40. Accompanying them north was William's younger brother, John, who homesteaded, too, and raised 19 children there. None of the Rolfes were long for Whitehall, however; William and Louisa were gone by the mid-1890s, while John stuck it out to the turn of the century.

Born in 1829, William Smith also hailed from England. Arriving in Canada, he married Christine Dalgliesh, three years his senior. They received title to two lots in 1887 in McMurrich Township, which suggests they arrived around 1882. In 1894, they were granted another 80 hectares under Christine's maiden name. By the time William died in 1913, they had abandoned their unprofitable farm and moved away from Whitehall.

It was the White family who, through determination and hard work, and frankly, sheer numbers, left the greatest mark on the region.

William Arthur White was born and raised in Ireland. It was a turbulent time on the Emerald Isle, with people dying of starvation and disease during what became known as the Great Hunger, and with endemic religious strife between Protestants and Catholics. William's family often went hungry, and matters only grew worse when his father was killed in sectarian fighting in 1848. Aged around 14 at the time, William Arthur was thrust into the role of head of the family. His first major decision came five years later, when he booked tickets for himself, his mother, and his six younger sisters for Canada, leaving the heartbreak of Ireland behind.

The White family initially settled near Kimberley, in Euphrasia Township, Grey County, Canada West. In 1858, William married Elizabeth Ditty, born in Grey County around 1840. The couple enjoyed a measure of prosperity on their farm and were blessed with five sons and a daughter. Sadly, but as was all too common in this era, Elizabeth died giving birth to the last born, Arthur. She was only about 33 years old. Grieving, and

William Arthur White left his native Ireland with his family in the 1850s, fleeing starvation and sectarian violence, the latter claiming his father. Even though William wasn't the first to settle in McMurrich Township, Whitehall was named in his honour, or, more specifically, after the hall he built to house the Orange Lodge and community events.

realizing he couldn't raise a baby on his own, William gave Arthur up to be cared for by his sister-in-law.

A few years later, William remarried, finding comfort, companionship, and a new mother, 19-year-old Christina McAllister, for his five at-home children. William and Christina had 10 children together, seven of them after the move to McMurrich Township. Indeed, it was very likely that it was this swelling family and the need to provide for them and leave property upon his death that spurred William to uproot from the established farm in Grey County and strike out for Parry Sound District, where land was plentiful. He was also encouraged by reports sent back from his sister, Jane, and her husband, John Bacon, who had made the move several years prior.

In 1879, William Arthur and his three eldest sons, William Hilliard, Thomas, and Robert, boarded the steamer *Waubuno* — a vessel that later mysteriously disappeared on Georgian Bay — at Collingwood and sailed north to Parry Sound. They then walked 64 kilometres east along a rough trail cut through the bush to reach McMurrich Township. William Arthur chose a lot in Concession 11 to homestead. The men spent the next two years building a cabin of pine logs, clearing land, and working spring through autumn, then returning to Kimberley before the snow fell. Finally, in the summer of 1881, Christina and the balance of the White children came north, reuniting the family permanently.

Now it was the turn of William Hilliard, Thomas, and Robert to select lots of their own. William Hilliard claimed plots southwest of his father's homestead, while Thomas settled on 120 hectares to the immediate east and Robert chose 40 hectares southeast of his father's farm. Robert was arguably the most successful of these elder sons. He was named pathmaster — responsible for the care of public paths and roads and ensuring annual mandatory road labour was done by property owners — in McMurrich Township in 1911 and 1916 and was elected councillor three times (1915, 1917, and 1918).

Nor was that the end of the White fiefdom in McMurrich. Christina claimed her own 40-hectare parcel, adding the land to her husband's holdings, while their daughter, Anna Elizabeth, homesteaded 40 hectares with her husband, William Briggs.

The Rolfes, Smiths, and Whites were hardly alone in settling this part of McMurrich. Others joined them, most of English, Scottish, or Irish descent. Some stayed longer than others, but all were united in a belief that homesteading represented an opportunity for a better future.

At first, Whitehall was nothing more than pockets of roughly cleared bush tied together by equally crude paths masquerading as roads. Life was anything but easy. And yet, in due time, the semblance of a community took form.

With no church or hall, there was nowhere for settlers to gather and develop the tight bonds for which small communities were known. Many people noted this glaring inadequacy, but it was Arthur White who acted. Around 1885, he built a public hall on his property that was utilized for dances, festivities, and communal meetings. William had no idea what the implication of this act of generosity would be. People began to speak of going to White's hall for one function or the other. It became a landmark, a focal point in an area with few and in a community without a name. Eventually, residents referred to the settlement as White's hall, which in time evolved into Whitehall. Ironically, despite its name, the hall was clad in red siding.

William was an ardent Protestant who proudly told anyone who would listen that his ancestor and namesake had proudly fought in the 1690 Battle of the Boyne, a victory over Irish Catholics lionized by Orangemen. He gathered like-minded men to establish an Orange Lodge, the only one ever in McMurrich Township. Naturally, the brethren held meetings in White's newly built hall.

By 1889, enough people had settled in this corner of McMurrich Township that a post office was warranted. It opened under Grosvenor Peale Brooks, a young man of about 28, on March 1. Brooks didn't hold the position long — he moved to Perry Township later that year — and so William White stepped in to fill the role. In these early years, mail was slow to arrive, coming via a circuitous route by train to Gravenhurst, steamship to Rosseau, and the stagecoach up Nipissing Road. William served as postmaster for 15 years until his death in 1904 and was followed by his widow, Christina, for another 14 years.

The arrival of the Ottawa, Arnprior, and Parry Sound Railway (OA&PSR) in 1891 changed everything in Whitehall, not the least the speed with which mail was delivered. The railway created a link to "civilization," relieving the oppressive sense of isolation settlers lived under and allowing logging companies to begin eyeing the area. Indeed, the benefit was felt even before the first train arrived, since local farmers profited by selling produce to the small army of labourers carving the rail line out of the bush. The White family gained most of all: in addition to selling farm produce, William Hilliard and Thomas were contracted to cut back the trees over the route the tracks took, while their father was hired as foreman for the construction of the railbed through McMurrich. Perhaps it was only fair that the White family reaped the benefits, since the tracks crossed the properties of several members of the extended family.

By 1894, the rail lines were complete and trains were running. The OA&PSR built a station at Whitehall, and the hamlet became a primary

The arrival of the Ottawa, Arnprior, and Parry Sound Railway in 1894 changed everything for Whitehall. It ended the sense of isolation that residents felt, sped up mail delivery, and most importantly, provided an avenue to ship logs to market. The lumber industry sustained Whitehall through much of its existence. The station was closed in 1945.

shipping terminal for timber. Sixteen sawmills were soon up and running in McMurrich, the cut lumber from which all went to market via Whitehall. Not every log was milled locally; thousands were shipped annually to be cut into lumber elsewhere. Additionally, a seemingly inexhaustible supply of tanbark was sent to the tannery in Huntsville. The forest was certainly good to the people of Whitehall.

The railway even attracted small-scale industry. Like so many homesteaders across the Canadian Shield, Samuel Sherk was frustrated with the meagre gains from his farm. But what if he could take advantage of the yellow birch that grew in thick stands all over his lot and those of his neighbours? Inspired, he opened a small factory producing birch veneer and basket bottoms. While it didn't make him rich, the enterprise lined his pockets with more money than he'd ever seen previously.

Although Whitehall derived most of its fortunes from harvesting the forest's resources, through ingenuity and gruelling work, homesteaders found a measure of success farming, as well. "As the land was cleared of trees and the farms increased in size," Iva Irwin (née White) wrote, "wheat, buckwheat, and oats were grown with great success. Peas, corn, barley, and rye were

Wheat was separated from chaff on a turn-of-the-century farm using a mechanical separator at centre and a steam engine at right. Steam engines were expensive, so typically a well-to-do landowner purchased one, then drove it from farm to farm, renting its services. The rocky nature of the landscape, evident in this photo, proved a challenge to farming in Whitehall.

successful, too." Iva was raised in the community, and as a young woman, taught at the community's school. With no gristmill in Whitehall, threshed grain had to be taken to Beggsboro to be ground into meal and flour.

"Potatoes and root crops grew bountiful," Iva recorded. "Planting potatoes was always done on the 24th of May holiday, weather permitting. Dad walking ahead with the plough, the children behind dropped the potato piece into the furrows, then the furrow was ploughed back over. Everyone looked forward to new potatoes for the 12th of July." Families also had large gardens for growing vegetables, and somewhat surprisingly, Iva noted that "currants, gooseberries, strawberries, and grapes grew to perfection."

In October 1913, School Section (SS) No. 4 McMurrich Township was announced in response to the growing number of youths in Whitehall. The following August, recently widowed Christina White donated half a hectare for the school. Her sons, William Hilliard and Robert, served as trustees alongside Samuel Phillips and treasurer E.C. Brownhill. George Rosger was contracted to build the school and outhouses for the sum of $1,040, while Carl Falstrom was paid $405 for the concrete foundations and a well.

Whitehall School Section (SS) No. 4 McMurrich Township was built in record time in 1914. The contract for its construction was signed on July 29, and students were attending classes by the first week of October. Centralized schooling and plummeting attendance saw the school close in 1943.

The school was completed in haste, opening October 12, 1914, with 16 pupils in attendance. The first teacher was Mary Bridget Cosgrove at a salary of $450 annually, but she lasted only until January and was replaced by William Mills. Such short tenures were hardly unusual at Whitehall; there were eight teachers in five years, most employed for a single semester. The one sense of continuity was William Hilliard White, who served as secretary-treasurer of the school board from 1916 until its closure three decades later.

A church was erected around the same time the school was built. Prior to that, a Methodist clergyman, Reverend McKay, hopped a train for Whitehall and held Sunday services right in the station. He was on the train that followed, off to his next ministry as soon as the service was over. Finally, Whitehall residents came together to raise a dedicated House of God, a place more conducive to prayer and thoughtful contemplation. The church that emerged was located just east of Whitehall. Originally Methodist, it later became Baptist under Reverend Widdifield, a resident of Whitehall.

Unlike so much of Whitehall that in time faded into history with nary a whimper, the church went out in dramatic fashion. One night, lightning illuminated the sky and struck the church. The subsequent flash that residents saw was the glow of fire in the evening sky. Before anyone could act, the church was engulfed in flames and burned down. There was never any thought of rebuilding it.

Churchgoers undoubtedly turned a blind eye to the illegal distilleries operating in Whitehall during the 1920s, one on the farm of lifelong bachelor Nick de George and another on John Hamilton's property. Even after Prohibition was repealed in 1927, the two men continued making a profit from the sale of homemade hooch well into the 1930s.

While logging in the region was done under the auspices of several lumber companies, the only sawmill of any size in Whitehall was owned and operated by Edgar White, Thomas's son. Born in 1908, Edgar was still a preteen when he went into the bush for the first time to cut trees during the winter. He became as comfortable in a logging camp or sawmill as in his own home.

Edgar was still a young man when he started the sawmill, located on the northwest corner of what is now Highway 518 and the road north to Bourdeau, but his years of experience served him well and the business thrived. The mill was a godsend in the dark days of the Depression, providing welcome employment for many local men. Logs by the thousand were piled nearby, ready to be cut into lumber. And it wasn't just men who benefited from the sawmill. "Hundreds and hundreds of cords of wood piled eight feet high were a perfect spot for the children to play hide-and-seek," remembered Iva Irwin.

Iva recalled one event, an episode of levity involving Edgar's lumbering venture. "In the spring of 1940, Edgar purchased eight two-year-old steers, some were red, and some were all black. They were to provide the meat for the men he had hired to work in the bush and at his mill during the winter months. When he arrived with them to Whitehall, he put them in the field to pasture. The cattle unfortunately were not accustomed to traffic and trains and ran away. The men spent hours tracking these cattle through the bush with no success. Everyone soon heard about the lost and wild cattle, but they were not seen by anyone."

Edgar White was a career logging man who first went into the bush as a preteen, felling trees at a lumber camp. Later, he operated this sawmill, which kept many men gainfully employed during the dark days of the Great Depression. In 1945, shortly after the closing of the railway and the only means of getting lumber to market, Edgar moved his operation to South River.

Six weeks later, the cattle were spotted hiding in the bush, but they had grown wild by this time and extremely skittish. As soon as anyone approached, they bolted. Determined to capture his cattle, Edgar gathered men for a roundup bee. "It was on a Sunday, so the women went along bringing a picnic lunch to watch the event," Iva wrote. "It was quite an experience, cornering these cattle and loading them onto a truck. They were certainly nice and fat when they were captured." A year prior, Edgar had married Grace Willett, a local lass. They resided in a large white home across from the mill on the northeast corner of the intersection.

There was a series of general stores in Whitehall during the community's history, though the first didn't appear until after the dawn of the 20th century when Peterborough-born Thomas Parker and his wife, Isabella, opened one in their home. The business ran for a decade or so through the early 1900s.

Next up were Edward and Anna Eliza Rhamey, who likewise ran a store from their home for a time. Anna Eliza, one of William White's numerous grandchildren and the daughter of William and Anne Briggs, managed the store quite nicely while Edward farmed, logged, and worked on the railway. When Anna Eliza died, age 34, in 1929, Edward didn't know what to do with the store, or frankly, himself, so he sold the home and business to William Hilliard White. William was postmaster from that time until his death in 1934, but again it was his wife, Dorothy, who ran the business. Upon William's passing, Dorothy stepped in as postmaster for three years.

In 1937, Edgar White purchased the house from his aunt and took over the job of postmaster. But he was too busy running his sawmill to spend much time on postal duties, so he passed the task to his sister, Muriel, who was de facto postmaster until 1944. She operated out of Whitehall's final general store, which was owned and operated by her parents.

In 1925, Thomas White built a new brick home on the site where his father had erected the first family cabin half a century earlier. From this sizable building, he and his wife, Sarah, ran a general store selling groceries and hardware, as well as seed and feed for area farmers. They installed a gas pump and had a telephone connected, in both cases novelties in the region. When Edgar was made postmaster and Muriel his stand-in, the post office was moved into their store. There was no hotel in Whitehall, so Thomas and Sarah opened their home as a boarding house serving travellers in need of beds for the night as well as schoolteachers requiring longer-term residence.

"The general store was typical of that time and stocked a variety of goods needed," remembers Merv Brown, who grew up in Parry Sound District in the 1930s and visited Whitehall often. "Of course, I remember the mandatory jars of hard candy on the counter that pennies could buy. If the proprietor was in a good mood, you might get a free one."

While Merv fantasized over candy on store shelves, Iva Irwin's eyes were drawn elsewhere: "Native women came from the Parry Sound Reserve [Wasauksing First Nation] with large packs on their backs full of all their fancy jewellery and baskets, baskets of all sizes for different uses. Many times, these women had a couple of meals at our home and stayed over-night." The women of Whitehall had great respect for the talent of these

Thomas and Sarah White operated this false-fronted general store from 1925 to 1947. This photo dates to the time of construction. The girl at left, Muriel White, served as postmaster in the late 1930s as a teenager.

Anishinaabeg artisans, and their ornate handcrafted baskets and jewellery were prized.

Whitehall was never large; at its peak, it was probably home to fewer than 50 people, a somewhat greater number when the people on the farms spreading out beyond the tiny core were added. As a result, the hamlet keenly felt any loss. When people slowly began drifting away in the 1920s and 1930s with their spirits and bodies broken by decades of hard work, it undermined the long-term prospects of the community. A plummeting population saw the school closed in 1943, with the task of locking the door falling to Mae Goss, the final teacher.

Edgar White wound up the sawmill two years later, the same time the railway station was shut down. He moved his operation to South River, where trains still regularly stopped and where timber and the labour force to

Pictured here in their wedding photo are Thomas White and Sarah Jane Hewitt, leading figures in 20th-century Whitehall. Thomas farmed and managed the hamlet's train station. Together, they operated the village general store and opened their home to boarders, including schoolteachers.

cut it were more plentiful. Most of the residents of Whitehall then worked for Edgar, so when he moved, it was a devastating blow. Many of the families followed him to South River and continued to work for him. By this time, Whitehall, never more than a blink-and-you'll-miss-it hamlet, was a shadow of its former self. In 1947, the post office closed, as well.

In the near seven decades since, nature has undone the work of Whitehall's settlers. Fields where grain once swayed in the wind and in which farmers dug for potatoes have become overgrown with regenerated forest. Many of the barns and homes slowly collapsed with the passage of years; today, few survive. Some one-time farms now boast modern homes, while others are indistinguishable from the bush, and only through painstaking search can one find evidence of past habitation in the form of foundations, wells, and stone fencing.

The false-fronted store, which operated until the late 1950s, still stands as a ghostly relic of Whitehall's past. It's a private residence today. Nearby runs the old roadbed of the Grand Trunk Railway, now a popular all-season recreational trail. A hike along a length of it provides some idea of the effort required to run this line across Central Ontario.

And what of the White family that lent its name to this hamlet? Several members, including William Arthur and Christina, slumber in Pioneer Cemetery, north of Sprucedale.

 To Get There

Whitehall huddles along Highway 518 in the middle of Parry Sound District, about 20 kilometres west of Highway 11 and a couple of kilometres west of Sprucedale. Sprucedale Pioneer Cemetery is northwest of Sprucedale at the end of Cemetery Road. With its aged and leaning headstones poking from the ground like wayward teeth, it's a haunting and sombre location. One feels the weight of the ages.

8

ROYSTON

(Ryerson Township, Parry Sound District)

I n the late 1870s, land-hungry settlers descended upon Ryerson Township, seeking a better life in the vastness of Ontario. They were lured there by the promise of 40-hectare lots for a single person, male or female, or 80 hectares for the head of a family, which would be theirs after five years of continuous settlement and upon clearing and improving four hectares of land.

Settlers had every reason to anticipate success. Government surveyor J.B. Clements had, after all, pronounced that Ryerson was ideal for agriculture, writing that the land was "generally of a sandy loam, light on the immediate surface, but becoming more rich as you dig deeper, with a fine subsoil of clay.... I consider there is seventy percent of arable land in the township." This was cruelly misleading, but prospective homesteaders didn't know that before heading north.

Upon arriving on their bush lots, settlers were stunned at how thickly forested the landscape was, how studded it was with rocks, and how infertile the soil appeared. Everything seemed daunting, frightening. Nonetheless, settlers gamely set about the task of establishing new homes for their

Government surveyor J.B. Clements insisted that 70 percent of Ryerson Township was fit for agriculture. He was wrong. Settlers cleared away the forest to find the soil barren and studded with rocks. Nonetheless, they gamely set about transforming the bush into farms. Eventually, the roads around Royston were lined with farmsteads, very much like the George Alexander spread pictured here.

families. They felled trees, built log cabins, and ploughed fields for crops. In the early years, most families felt as if they were in an endless battle just to make ends meet. Life was hard. Many days there was little more than cornbread and beans, perhaps some game, to eat. But thankfully there was the logging industry.

Ryerson Township was witnessing a logging boom. Thick stands of pine lured lumber companies into the region, and men with strong arms and stronger backs were needed to cut the towering trees. The struggling home-steaders were only too willing to spend their winters in logging camps for the promise of good pay and decent food. Money brought home from these months away sustained many families through lean years, granting bush farms a chance to establish roots and grow.

Slowly, almost imperceptibly at first, a village began to develop, cen-tred on the crossroads of what became Royston Road and Doe Lake Road (now Stisted Road). The first hint of community — beyond scattered bush farms — was a one-room log schoolhouse, School Section (SS) No. 2, raised in 1871 to see to the education of local children. Measuring a mere five by seven metres, the school was primitive in the extreme, with children sitting on split log benches with no backrests and with boards painted dark in lieu of a blackboard. The developing hamlet became known as Royston, honouring the homesteading Roy family.

George and Eliza Roy arrived in Ryerson Township around 1869, at the forefront of settlement. Although a skilled wheelwright, Roy didn't seem to practise his trade after arriving in Parry Sound District. There simply weren't enough people in the region to create any demand. What there was a call for, however, was cut lumber with which to build homes, barns, and furniture. With that in mind, Roy launched a sawmill just south of Royston Road and beside Doe Lake Road. To ensure a steady, year-round flow of water to power the mill, Royston Creek was dammed. Like all settlers, the Roys also cultivated their land.

Although the community was named after George Roy, few could compete with George Todd for local pre-eminence. Todd had already lived a life before arriving in Ryerson. Born in Carmylie, Scotland, in 1820, he and his wife, Mary, packed up their four children and sailed to Canada in 1853. They settled at first in Luther Township, where George, a cobbler and farmer, gained the respect of his neighbours and became the township's reeve. Around 1873, George and Mary, accompanied by their adult sons, William and Alexander, packed up once more and headed north for Parry Sound District.

Todd once again established himself as a prominent figure and leading voice in his community. While farming to provide for his family, he also plied his trade from a room in the front of the home. Far from just making shoes, George did all manner of leather work — harnesses and reins, saddles, even leather drive belts for steam-driven pulleys. Todd served as a school trustee and was elected Ryerson Township's first reeve on March 13, 1880.

Although long in the shadow of his father, William Sheriff Todd was very much his own man. As a 17-year-old in 1870, he had served in the militia to defend the young nation from Irish nationalist Fenian raids launched from the United States. Then, in Royston, he farmed, worked as a carpenter and builder, notably erecting three schoolhouses in the area (Doe Lake in 1891, Wiseman in 1893, and Midlothian in 1898), was made constable in

1880 with an annual salary of $2, and served as a member of the Ryerson Township Council. William and his wife, Charlotte, also found time to raise seven children.

Charlotte's parents, Irish-born John and Ann Nelson, were also esteemed voices in the community. After arriving in Canada in the early 1850s, they farmed for several decades near Grand Valley in Ontario before accompanying the Todd family north to Parry Sound District. As such, John and Ann were among the earliest settlers in Royston, and somehow, with the assistance of their four as-yet unwed daughters, turned their bush lot into a productive farm. Indeed, while the original log home burned down in 1924, the farm remained in the family for more than a century. John also became a long-time reeve of Ryerson Township.

For much of its early existence, roads linking Royston to the outside world were circuitous and in poor repair. Instead, travel along the Magnetawan River was preferred. The steamship *Armour* sailed daily from Burk's Falls, which had rail access to points as far west as Ahmic Harbour. One stop along the route was Younger's Landing, just north of Royston proper and named for Charles Younger.

While the Royston of the 1870s still wasn't a particularly large settlement, not even the biggest in Ryerson Township, it developed into the township's travel hub. There was no road link to Burk's Falls, despite being only a few kilometres distant, and getting to Magnetawan by land was via a lengthy, winding road that was still rather primitive. A far more convenient and comfortable means of reaching either town was to travel north through Royston to the Magnetawan River and there catch a steamboat from the wharf at Younger's Landing, named for Charles Younger, who as a 60-year-old in 1871 had settled along the river with his wife. Over time, existing roads naturally improved and new ones were built. Most important was Midlothian Road, running east to Burk's Falls and opening for traffic in 1883. Yet the landing remained a vital transportation link, since the movement of goods and personal travel remained more efficient by steamboat than by rattling wagon.

The year 1885 was an important one for Royston. That summer, railway navvies finished laying the tracks of the Grand Trunk Railway from Huntsville north to Burk's Falls, about eight kilometres northwest of Royston. Overnight, Burk's Falls grew into a thriving transportation hub. Spurred by an easy means of getting cut timber to distant markets, logging companies redoubled their efforts throughout the region. Logs by the hundreds were shipped up the Magnetawan River to Burk's Falls, which was a boon for Royston and its residents, sparking a heady decade for the village.

It was around this time that George Alexander opened the doors to a general store, which was a welcome addition to the community since it meant settlers no longer had to venture farther afield to pick up provisions and purchase such wares as they could afford. Alexander, who was 60 years old when he greeted his first customer, eventually held an elevated status in Royston's social hierarchy, one he wasn't unfamiliar with.

The roots of the Alexander family were in Gloucester, England, where George, the son of an Anglican clergyman of some means, was born and raised in comfort. He received a fine education and married well; his wife, Esther Floyd Wooster, was from another prominent family. With backing from his family and a sizable inheritance Esther brought with her to the marriage, the couple moved to London, where George set himself up as a

George Alexander was among Royston's earliest settlers and became one of its leading citizens. He opened the community's first general store and served as postmaster, reclaiming some of the prominence he lost when the family left England. His passing in 1905 was deeply felt in Royston.

draper, making and selling cloth. The Alexanders did well for themselves. They were blessed with a large home and the comforts of numerous servants, including a governess to help look after a growing family. Eventually, there were 11 children in all.

For reasons that no one can explain but likely had to do with a business failure, George and Esther packed up their family in 1878, boarded the SS *Sarmatian*, and headed for Canada. They ended up in Ryerson Township, farming a homestead, all luxury and refinement seemingly a lifetime in the past. But even in the bush of Parry Sound District, George's ambition remained undimmed. As soon as there were enough settlers in the area, he opened a general store. It paled in comparison to the business he left behind in England, but it offered him a reprieve from the back-breaking toil of operating a bush farm and was certainly far more lucrative. In 1890, Alexander received a postal contract, another feather in his cap. He was a man of prominence again.

The following year, Royston's residents decided the old school had had its day. It was drafty and the roof leaked, and enrollment was now averaging 50 students, far too many for the postage stamp–sized building. The

Esther Alexander, George Alexander's wife, is seen here with her two eldest daughters. She was an unlikely pioneer who was born in comfort in England. Esther used the sizable inheritance she brought to the marriage to help George set up a cloth wholesale and retail business in London. They were blessed with a large home and the luxury of numerous servants, including a governess to help look after an expanding family. All these trappings of wealth were left behind when the family sailed for Canada and a future in Parry Sound District.

community pooled its resources, financial and labour alike, to raise SS No. 2 Ryerson, a new frame schoolhouse. Larger and far better outfitted, the new school was, observers noted, something the community could be proud of. "The school is a model," wrote Baptist minister J. Blatherwick, who observed classes on June 11, 1891. "Good house, good teacher, good attendance and work." George W. Young, from McMaster University, came to much the same conclusion when he visited two years later. "I have had the pleasure of visiting this school for a few minutes today and was never more impressed with the excellent order and true sympathy of teacher toward the scholars."

Spiritual needs for the community were addressed by a trio of churches. A Presbyterian one stood on Royston Road across from the cemetery. The pride and joy of the 16-member congregation was an ornate little organ that when played by Mrs. Ilman "never failed to lift the voices of those who worshipped within the Presbyterian walls." The organist was forced to entertain restless congregants when the minister was late in arriving, an all-too-frequent occurrence. The reason behind his tardiness became a fondly told local tale. There was a hill just across the bridge crossing Royston Creek that the minister's horse balked at climbing. The frustrated clergyman had to use every trick in the book to coax the horse up the hill, frequently making him late for service. That hill became known as Balky Hill.

Just south of the school stood a Baptist church. Originally built of logs, it was replaced in 1891 by a frame structure. Parishioners invested heavily in the church, installing beautiful stained-glass windows on the north and south walls, which had both practical and spiritual purposes. The windows provided illumination, but more than that, the coloured light that filtered in made churchgoers believe they were in the presence of God. A driving shed with a capacity for more than a dozen teams was built at the same time.

The final church, catering to Methodists, stood at the southeast corner of the village crossroads, next door to the Todd home. The congregation was

The spiritual needs of Royston's settlers were catered to by a trio of churches — Methodist, Baptist, and Presbyterian. The Baptist church was located just south of the school. Originally built of logs, it was replaced with this handsome frame structure in 1891. It burned down around 1952.

formed in 1879, but for a decade, church service was held in private homes or outdoors when the weather was fine. A log church was finally built, then replaced in 1897 by a finer frame structure.

Loyal Orange Lodge (LOL) No. 929 opened in 1894, serving as a community hall for social functions ranging from weddings and quilting bees to school Christmas concerts and dances. Soon, a second general store was opened, offering competition to George Alexander's. The quiet of the forests and fields was now pierced by the whine of saw blades. William James Shea, born in Grimsby on Lake Ontario half a century earlier, built a steam-powered sawmill along the river. With Royston experiencing a growth spurt and residents upgrading their residences from log cabins to better plank homes as the community matured out of its frontier state, there was a ready market for lumber, which Shea met. Indeed, to profit from it, he had a huge boiler brought in by steamboat, poured huge concrete blocks to place it upon, and set about cutting lumber. He must have done well for himself, since the census shows the family had a live-in servant.

In addition to numerous farms, Royston at its peak boasted a mill, a store, a smithy, a school, a Loyal Orange Lodge, three churches, and this handsome manse to house the Baptist minister. Royston was the commercial and social hub of Ryerson Township.

By this point, Royston had become the social and commercial centre for Ryerson Township, surpassing nearby communities such as Starrat and Doe Lake in importance. All roads seemed to lead to Royston. The community was thriving in a way those initial settlers could only have dreamed of, hoped for, when fighting off hunger pangs two decades earlier.

The dawn of the new century was greeted with optimism by the folk of Royston, certain that even greater things were in store. They couldn't have been more wrong. The first blows were the loss of several village stalwarts. As his wife, Mary Ann, and their three children stood by his bedside, William Shea died in February 1904. Later that year, in September, George Alexander passed away, as well, the victim of a sudden heart attack at 74. But at least he died knowing his general store would continue, first under his wife, Esther, then from 1906 to 1909 under their daughter and son-in-law, Esther and Robert Clark. John Nelson, who was always a guiding hand in the community — "he always took a keen and active interest in public affairs," noted his obituary in the *Burk's Falls Arrow* — died in 1907. So, one by one, the stalwart individuals who had established the community and who for decades had been the glue that bonded it together were taken away.

The passing of these men coincided with the sliding fortunes of Royston. Many residents, exhausted and dispirited from years of investing so much into farms that gave so little in return, threw up their hands in defeat and left for greener pastures. That this happened at the same time as widespread logging in Ryerson Township was winding down is no coincidence — logging had been the foundation upon which Royston had been built. Arthur James Alexander, the youngest son of George and Esther, took over the Shea sawmill and ran it for a few more years with diminishing returns before winding up the operation. The Roy family wasn't immune to the changes causing such uncertainty. Shortly after the turn of the century, they said goodbye to the community that bore their name and moved westward to Spence Township, where George raised a new sawmill. The youngest son, James Melvin, joined him. The loss of these two sawmills and the jobs and market for timber from bush lots they represented hurt those people remaining in Royston.

Royston's future became even bleaker in the aftermath of the First World War. Some of the young men who served overseas during the conflict chose not to return to the village upon their return. Exposed to the wider world, Royston seemed small and insignificant.

The first victim of communal atrophy was the school, which closed in 1918. After that, children were bused to school in Burk's Falls. The post office contract was pulled from Art Alexander in 1923, which was a significant blow to the general store. Reduced foot traffic impacted sales, contributing to his decision a few years later, painful as it was, to close the store his father had started. Now a second of the community's pillars was gone.

Shrinking congregations saw the Presbyterians and Methodists amalgamate to form the United Church in 1925. This only put off the inevitable by a decade; in 1937, the United Church was closed and its lumber auctioned off. By this time, the old Presbyterian church had been gone for seven years, also torn down to salvage the wood. The Baptist church was the last to go, enduring until 1943, when the congregation cried through a final sermon. The church sat empty for a while but burned down around 1952. It represented the last reminder of community.

Today, Royston has the look of just another country road. Much has changed in the century plus since the village was a going concern in Ryerson Township. Sideroads have disappeared, farms are overgrown, and even Royston Creek has largely dried up and almost disappeared. It can be difficult to orient oneself and visualize the village in the mind's eye.

Some firm evidence of Royston remains, though. Here and there stand still-inhabited period homes, but they're so spaced apart they do nothing to hint that a thriving community once existed here. Nevertheless, the old crossroads village does offer some ghosts. The Royston cemetery stands without its church, the former schoolhouse, where generations of children learned the three Rs, is now a private residence, and in the regenerated forests lurk shells and overgrown foundations representing shadowy remnants of a forgotten past.

To Get There

Take Peggs Mountain Road west from the village of Burk's Falls, then turn west onto Royston Road. The one-time farm village is stretched along this road, principally centred around the intersection of Royston and Stisted Roads.

9

SPENCE

(Spence Township, Parry Sound District)

Spence is tucked into the recesses of Parry Sound District, located along the old Nipissing Colonization Road. In its day, the village was a thriving community, but today it's more ghost than town. Its few remaining crumbling edifices belie a remarkably resilient farming community that survived, if not ever truly thriving, for half a century.

The promise of free land drew thousands of land-hungry settlers into Parry Sound District in the latter years of the 19th century, when the Nipissing Colonization Road was cut through the bush and forests from Lake Rosseau in the south to Lake Nipissing in the north. Along its length in the 1860s, hopeful pioneers carved out farms, all part of a plan to open the region for logging concerns. Settlement of the region was a vital prerequisite for logging, since it provided a ready source of men with strong backs eager for work, of horses to pull logs to frozen rivers in preparation for spring log drives, and of barley and potatoes to feed people and horses alike. Without settlers, logging operations would have been costly and difficult. Thus, the Ontario government passed the Free Grant and Homestead Act in

1868, offering free lots to anyone willing to put down roots in Parry Sound District. The proposition drew flocks of land-hungry settlers, some of whom were the founders of Spence.

After disembarking from steamers in Parry Sound, these hopeful families trudged along rutted roads to take up their allotments, carrying their worldly possessions in wagons and on their backs. In his later years, James Alexander Bell, the youngest son of settler Isaac Bell, recalled the family's arrival in Spence Township. At nine years of age, he was responsible for herding sheep from Parry Sound to the homestead location and keeping them safe from forest predators. His elder sister, Ellen, led a cow at the head of the family convoy so that the remainder of the cattle followed. James remembered stopping along the way to feed the animals at small beaver meadows where enterprising newcomers had gone ahead and cut beaver hay — grass that grew wild in beaver meadows — to sell to the settlers as they passed through. In a land where forests encroached on all sides, where else could one find forage for livestock until the land was cleared?

Spence owed its existence to traffic along Nipissing Road, which stretched from Cameron Bay on Lake Rosseau in the south to Lake Nipissing in the north. Maintaining and improving the road was the responsibility of area farmers who had to turn out for several days of statute labour each year.

People made do. The Nelson family, arriving around the same time as the Bells, sheltered for months in a piggery owned by Isaac "Old Man" Brown, who had preceded them by a year or two. The pigs were temporarily moved out, fresh straw was laid on the ground, and hastily built bunks with evergreen bough mattresses were brought in. Many settlers weren't even that fortunate and spent weeks or months sleeping in tents or wagons until shanties could be built.

With the arrival of the Bells, Nelsons, and other families like them, the hamlet of Spence sprang up as suddenly as a trillium in a springtime forest. Named for Robert Spence, the postmaster general of the Province of Canada from 1854 to 1857, and located at the intersection of the Ryerson Colonization Road (now North Lake Road), it boasted the amenities found in most farming communities, including a general store, a post office, a blacksmith shop, a couple of sawmills, a church, several carpenters, and a

The first Spence school was opened in 1875, later replaced with this frame school, which still stands. Among the noteworthy early teachers was Hamilton Brown, standing in the back row in this 1885 photo, who earned a reputation as a very progressive educator, first on Manitoulin Island and then in Spence. Brown was also a farmer and postmaster during his time in Spence.

Loyal Orange Lodge. At Spence's peak, 150 people proudly called it home, each one motivated by a desire to plant feet on land they could call their own, a goal they could never achieve in their native Britain or Ireland.

Henry Brown donated one-fifth of a hectare of his farm for the erection of a log schoolhouse. Opened in March 1875, it measured six by nine metres. The schoolhouse was quirky and somewhat primitive — pine boards painted over with black paint served as chalkboards, for example.

The local church was the focal point of communal pride in most rural communities, and Spence was no different. In the first few years, while settlers struggled to establish new farms and new lives, church services were held in the schoolhouse. By 1884, however, the foundations of the community had been laid and residents pooled their resources to build a dedicated house of worship. Gilbert McCracken donated land, and men went into the bush to cut trees that were then pulled out by horses and oxen to a sawmill, where the logs were milled into lumber. There was little money for nails or

In 1884, the Spence church was built on land donated by Gilbert McCracken. On each side facing the altar were little wooden pews seating three people. The middle was furnished with several long bench-type seats for about six, which originally had been in train cars.

windows, so work lagged. The first service was held that Christmas, even though lack of money meant the church was still not finished.

Reba Garnett (née Keppy), who was born in Spence in 1925 and resided there until 1942, left us with a recollection of the church so evocative that it suggests her heart never truly left the little village:

> How vividly I recall the high frame building by Nipissing Road with an outer woodshed which doubled as a drive shed for the horses and conveyances in the winter. A lean-to shed had been built at the back of the church and served useful, equipped with wood-burning cook stove, tables, and a bookcase. It was used as a dressing room at the annual Christmas concert. The interior of the sanctuary, with its gothic type windows, seemed very impressive. The hanging coal-oil lamps with their pretty flowered glass shades to me were elegance personified. When they were alight at evening services, I thought, *This must be like heaven.*

Amos and Elizabeth Keppy are pictured here on their way to church in 1938. Sleighs remained the principal means of winter travel into the 1940s, since roads were unploughed and snow was often piled as high as power lines. Amos was extremely pious and came by that honestly; his father, Robert, was one of the movers behind establishing Spence's church.

The largest building in Spence and its most prosperous business was the roadside inn built in 1878 by Levitt Simpson, a 54-year-old gentleman who had just recently stepped off a ship from his native England. With his wife, Ann, and four children in tow, he headed for Parry Sound District to take up a new life as a hotelier. The inn catered primarily to road-weary travellers passing through, and because it was located roughly at the midway point of Nipissing Road, Simpson named the establishment the Halfway House. It was somewhere people could find refreshment, stabling for exhausted horses, and a place to sleep for the night.

Life in Spence wasn't easy. Luxuries were few, and though the soil was rocky and infertile, the pioneers hoped that hard work in the summer would be enough to coax crops from the earth to feed their families, with perhaps a bit left over to sell.

In the winter, men and boys sought work at logging camps to supplement the meagre income from their farms. Merv Brown, who grew up on a hardscrabble Spence farm in the 1930s, recalled, "My dad, John, like most young boys at that time, intermittently attended public school for three or four years, then, at age 13, left home to drive a team of horses in a lumber camp. Horse-drawn sleighs were driven along Nipissing Road to sawmills at Canoe Lake, North Seguin, Bear Lake, Whitehall, and others. In later years, loads of lumber and tanbark were driven to the Grand Trunk station at Seguin Falls. As long as the lumber industry endured, people had a means of supporting themselves."

Hardships were many, tragedies common. Martha Langford, born in Spence in 1889, spoke later in life of wading through kilometres of snow to attend the one-room schoolhouse: "All the horses were away working in the bush in the winter, so we had to walk if we wanted to get there." Worse was to follow for the young girl. In the middle of the winter of 1902, a calf got out of the barn and stumbled into an icy brook. With her father away in a logging camp, Martha's pregnant mother was forced to wade into the freezing water to rescue the valuable calf. Unfortunately, the exertion caused Martha's mother to go into premature labour and give birth to a crippled and sickly son. With her mother and the newborn ill, 13-year-old Martha became woman of the house for much of the winter and had to take on a permanently increased role on the farm, never again returning to school.

The tragic story of Betsy Cairns reflects just how thin the line between life and death was in a backwoods community such as Spence. In 1873, Betsy and her husband, William, occupied a modest log cabin. William went off hunting one day to supplement the scanty food he'd harvested among the tree stumps of his farm, kissing his pregnant wife and infant daughter goodbye. He never returned, dying in a tragic shooting accident. Alone and with children to feed, Betsy didn't have the luxury of mourning William for long. Instead, she married George Ross and moved into his house, saying farewell to the cabin into which she and William had invested so much of their dreams for the future. Betsy decided to let her old farm become a village cemetery, with William as the first person interred there, in the corner of what was once the patch of forest he'd cleared to raise crops. Many of the headstones that followed bore similar tragic stories.

As with any community, Spence had its share of colourful characters. Local farmer Ned Glass was said to be something of a miracle worker. Reputedly, he could stop bleeding and had even been seen to save the life of a horse that had been badly, it was thought mortally, injured. And then there was Joe Glass, the fife player for the Orange Lodge for the annual July 12 parade. A lifelong bachelor, Joe wasn't particularly careful about his personal hygiene. A day or so before each parade day, the other lodge members took Joe down to Old Man's Creek and gave him a bath and shave. The wife of one of the members washed and pressed his uniform to make Joe more presentable.

The turn of the century brought a grim reversal of fortune for Spence. The 1900s weren't kind to the village and those who called it home. In 1896, the railway was extended from Huntsville to Callander on Lake Nipissing. With the opening of that line, traffic along Nipissing Road — the very foundation of Spence's prosperity — started to wither away. At the same time, the logging industry collapsed due to overharvesting, which deprived men of important wintertime employment. The surrounding population declined precipitously as a second generation abandoned the struggling farms inherited from their parents, preferring to walk away rather than endure the isolation and hardships of life on a bush farm. Those factors conspired to undermine Spence's health in the early decades of the 20th century so that with each passing year the village deteriorated more and more.

The hotel, of all the businesses in town, fell the farthest. Donald MacEachern, who took possession of it around 1890, watched in dismay as traffic along Nipissing Road petered out immediately after the railway was completed. He thought to stave off financial difficulties by adding a sizable barroom to the hotel, in which he served alcohol for the first time.

The Spence Inn closed in 1911, after which it served as a residence for a series of owners, including William and Effie Doherty from 1919. Because they lived closest to the school, the two Doherty girls, Evelyn and Olive (seen here with the hotel in the background), were expected to go early each morning to light a fire in the pot-bellied stove, stock the school with firewood, bring in drinking water from the well, and sweep the floors. For all that, they earned 75 cents a week.

MacEachern hoped, even perhaps prayed, he could replace tired travellers with local farmers willing to drown their sorrows over barren soil and harsh seasons with booze. It didn't work. While the hotel hung on for a time, with each passing year it became less profitable, and so by 1911, MacEachern finally tossed in the towel. To his credit, he survived longer than most businesses in town. The hotel thereafter served as a private residence for a series of individuals, beginning with Hamilton Brown, the long-time local schoolteacher who retired and took up farming.

Incredibly, even after the village began to falter, some people actually prospered in this cruel environment, thanks to tireless work and ingenuity. In 1921, Amos Keppy inherited the family farm founded two generations earlier. With knowledge and training he received while attending Ontario Agricultural College, he managed to make his farm thrive. The addition of a sawmill, as well, also helped him earn a very good living for himself and his family.

On September 24, 1872, Loyal Orange Lodge (LOL) 799 opened in Spence. The land was donated by David Nelson, the first worshipful master of the lodge. The hall wasn't just used for meetings of Orangemen but also for a range of community functions from dances to weddings. Baseball games were played in an adjacent field every Saturday throughout the summer. The building still stands.

Although life in Spence could be challenging, there were good times to be had — dances at the Orange Lodge, picnics after church, bake sales and bazaars, and bees where many hands made light work. But one event stood out, one for which calendars were circled with eager anticipation months in advance.

"The annual Christmas concert, in my mind, was the 'icing on the cake,'" suggested Reba Garnett:

> The pupils from Spence school, aptly trained by their teachers, would present a program that gave the community a seasonal lift. It was suitably referred to by many as "The Entertainment." The young people above school age would usually surprise us with more sophisticated numbers. Santa came and always found the children a gift and a bag of nuts and candies on or under the two towering spruce trees. As long as I live, I will never forget the magic of those evenings, fortified by the fragrance of the evergreens. Because Spence church was a Mission Charge, a huge box was sent to us from a Presbytery in Galt. We referred to it as the "Galt Box." It was filled with goodies, toys, and books for everyone, which solved Santa's problems. I cannot describe the anticipation when the Galt Box arrived by CNR.

Farms continued to cling to life well into the 20th century, almost in defiance of nature. They were, in the words of Merv Brown, a "hardscrabble lot." Even eight decades removed from his life of bundling hay and ploughing fields, Merv can still feel the ache of a tired back when reflecting on his youth. "It was a lot of hard work. When one grew up on a farm, you were expected to do what work you could handle — and a bit more. It was a matter of pride to be able to do 'grown-up' jobs. I believe Dad owned about six or seven hundred acres, with roughly one-third under cultivation and the rest bush. Like most everyone around, he grew hay, oats, barley, peas, potatoes, and turnips. Everyone raised pigs — a mix of barley and oats was ground into pig feed. Dad also had four horses and around 25 to 30 cows, which he had to hand-milk twice daily."

Merv hastened to mention his mother, whom he clearly adored, lest one think farming was man's work alone. "Mom enjoyed working outside coiling hay, milking cows, splitting firewood, and growing a large garden in addition to cooking, baking, canning, preserving, washing, cleaning, and raising a family. Mom would always bring us a snack and tea when we were working in the fields, which she would do mid-morning and mid-afternoon. She, like most farmwomen of the day, was one busy lady."

As time passed, farmers gradually gave up and moved on. The work was too hard, the reward too paltry. But even as the community shrank in the 20th century, Spence retained its school. The original log structure was long gone by then, replaced in 1909 by a fine wood-plank building. Viola Thomas (née Bell) remembered it well. "It was a one-room schoolhouse with a washroom in the front porch on the left, two pails of spring creek drinking water with dippers on the right, a wood stove directly as you walked in the front door. The teacher's desk to the left, blackboard to the right. The old creaky wooden floors supported about 15 students with little wooden desks.

The Spence school, class of 1935, under Donalda Reid, who came to Spence as a novice teacher in 1931 and probably anticipated remaining only a year, or perhaps two, like most of the young women before her. But she married local farmer Mel Brown and ended up staying and teaching in Spence for more than a decade.

In winter, the roads were not ploughed so my dad would break a trail with his horses and a homemade wooden snowplough so the kids could walk or ski to the schoolhouse."

By the eve of the Second World War, the farm population of Spence, diminishing since the turn of the century, virtually flatlined. Only a handful of stalwart families endured. In 1949, in what was a very sad day, the decision was made to close the school and bus children to nearby Magnetawan for classes. Even the Keppy homestead couldn't survive. Farm fields once filled with hay or swaying stalks of grain were reduced to weed-infested meadows.

Standing at the intersection of Nipissing and Blacks Roads today, it's difficult to imagine that a village existed here as recently as seven decades ago. The location is wrapped in a ghostly shroud. Old farm roads now disappear into trails in the bush, and most of the fields where crops once grew have long since been reclaimed by the forest. Only cellar holes and foundations remain to testify to the village's former extent and the vibrancy of life that existed here.

The ruined foundation of an old barn on the Bell family homestead speaks to both the community's agricultural past and its ultimate demise. Yet members of the family still farm the land today.

Close your eyes for a moment and try to visualize how it must have appeared: stagecoaches pulling up to the Halfway House on the northeast corner, where dusty, drowsy passengers climb down to stretch legs and find a warm meal; on the northwest corner, the general store and post office selling everything residents could possibly desire.

Elsewhere, the Orange Hall, enduring at the intersection of Nipissing and Ahmic Lake Roads, isn't slowly losing its long battle with time and the elements. Instead, in the imagination, it's tall and proud, fastidiously cared for by local men who once gathered there to share their love of community and religion. The one-time schoolhouse, School Section (SS) No. 1 Spence, still remains opposite Nelson Lake Road but now serves as a private residence. If one tries hard enough, Spence almost seems to come alive again.

And although Spence is no longer, this isn't a completely closed chapter in its history. The former Spence Inn, purchased in 1977 by the Rotary Club of Huntsville, was moved to Muskoka Heritage Place, and after extensive renovation, is a reminder of life in this long-gone roadside community. For

The Spence Inn survives. In a ruined state, it was purchased in 1977 by the Rotary Club of Huntsville, was moved to Muskoka Heritage Place, and was fully restored. It continues to serve the public 150 years after being built, now as a living-history reminder of the countless forgotten roadside inns that dotted cottage country in the 19th century.

as long as the former inn stands, the book on Spence remains open and the narrative of this resilient community can be shared.

 To Get There

Spence lies along Nipissing Road, south of Magnetawan. The core of the community was the intersection of Nipissing and Blacks Roads. The hotel stood on the northeast corner. Until recently, a historic sign marked its location, but it was stolen by vandals a few years ago.

PART THREE
- - - - - - - - - - - - -

Northern Cottage Country

BYNG INLET

(Wallbridge Township, Parry Sound District)

A century ago, Byng Inlet was one of the greatest lumber-producing communities in Ontario. At the time, the clamour of heavy industry was near-deafening, the sweet scent of freshly cut wood inescapable. But there is as much gravity as glory in the history of this former lumber town.

Byng Inlet was conceived on the promise of wealth. By the late 1860s, American lumbermen from Michigan, faced with the depletion of the once seemingly endless stands of white pine in their native state, cast their eyes across the Great Lakes to Ontario for new sources of timber. Logging rights were snapped up to keep their mills running. At the mouths of rivers all along the length of Georgian Bay, sawn logs driven down from the forested interior were corralled, encircled with booms, and then towed to Michigan.

In the summer of 1868, surveyor Vernon B. Wadsworth was dispatched by the Michigan-based Clarke, White and Co. to locate appropriate mill sites that might serve its newly acquired Magnetawan River timber rights. Wadsworth selected two spots on or near islets at the mouth of Byng Inlet. Here, the mills would be easily accessible by steamers in Georgian Bay and yet still be in a sheltered cove where logs could be collected after being rafted down from the interior highlands.

Two years later, Wadsworth returned to survey another mill location, this time for the Dodge Lumber Company, which also had timber rights along the Magnetawan headwaters. At the instruction of his employers, in addition to selecting a mill site, he also laid out an adjacent village plan, naming it after the inlet upon which it was located. In its earliest days, Byng Inlet was little more than a rough-and-tumble frontier camp where mill hands and their families existed in a sprawl of ramshackle cabins without sanitation or the niceties of civilization. It was hardly an Eden, and yet a vast fortune in lumber passed through on the way to markets in the United States, specifically that country's East Coast and Midwest.

Sometime during the early 1870s, the Dodge Company purchased the holdings of Clarke, White and Co., its rival. The demand for lumber was so great that one of Clarke, White's recently acquired mills was kept in operation to supplement Dodge's own facility. Dodge employed 160 employees at the two mills, producing 47,194 cubic metres per year.

In 1889, things began to unravel for Byng Inlet. With trouble brewing elsewhere in its business empire, Dodge started to divest itself of many of its far-flung holdings. The Byng Inlet operation was sold to Merrill and Ring, a lumber conglomerate based out of Saginaw, Michigan.

If the residents of Byng Inlet thought Merrill and Ring was riding to their rescue, breathing new life into a moribund community, their hopes were soon dashed. The firm had no interest in the well-being of an isolated Canadian village and its people; it had mill towns of its own in Michigan to worry about. Merrill and Ring opted to raft logs across Lake Huron to keep its Michigan mill humming, rather than cut timber at an Ontario sawmill. This decision rescued several American communities that had gone on life support when domestic sources of timber were exhausted, but it put hundreds of men out of work in Byng Inlet. Predictably, the community went into a period of steep decline, with most residents moving away to search for employment.

Ironically, Byng Inlet's salvation came courtesy of another Michigan-based lumber firm, Holland and Emery, and thanks to a nasty trade dispute between Canada and the United States. The Dingley Act, passed by the U.S. Congress in 1897 during the protectionist presidency of William McKinley, imposed a duty of $2 per 2.4 cubic metres on imported sawn timber. This was designed to keep American sawmills operating at the expense of Canadian ones, despite the fact that much of the lumber being used in the United States originated in Canada. Consequently, numerous Ontario sawmills sat idle or were forced to close outright. Desperate mill owners took their plight to Queen's Park in Toronto. To its credit, the Ontario government responded quickly, passing legislation that required all timber harvested on Crown lands in the province to be manufactured into sawn lumber within Ontario. There would be no more booming across the Great Lakes. The law came into effect on April 1, 1898.

Merrill and Ring, caught unprepared by the development, suddenly found itself cut off from its timber supply. Disgusted, the U.S. firm sold its Ontario holding to Holland and Emery, a company that operated mills near Bay City, Michigan. Holland and Emery closed the state-of-the-art mill in Bay City, dismantled it, and shipped it lock, stock, and barrel across Lake Huron to be reassembled at Byng Inlet. This sparked the growth of Byng

The Magnetawan River and its tributaries, which stretch as far inland as the Algonquin Highlands, was a highway by which logs were driven down to Byng Inlet each spring. Initially, logs were towed across Lake Huron in massive booms to be cut in Michigan. Later, the mills were relocated to Byng Inlet, giving rise to a thriving community.

Inlet, transforming it over the next few years into a prosperous community of several hundred souls.

The mill quickly became among the largest lumber operations in Ontario, employing hundreds of men and turning out 47.2 cubic metres daily. The facility consisted of two sawmills, state-of-the-art box and lathe factories, a planing mill, and a dry kiln. The boilers ran on sawdust, edgings, and other waste, while conveyor chains carried the fuel into the boilers. The mills, lumberyard, and boilers covered an area of more than 2.6 square kilometres. Cut lumber was towed away by horse-drawn wagons along an extensive network of tramways. "They had lumberyards by the mile," remembered Jack Laird, who worked at the mill. "I may be exaggerating, but I imagined there'd be four or five miles of tramways." All summer long an endless parade of steamers and schooners arrived in Byng Inlet to carry lumber to ports throughout the Great Lakes.

Mill hands lived in company-owned homes and boarding houses and did their shopping at a company store. Direct current electricity for domestic

A lumberyard at Byng Inlet, circa 1910. The mills ran around the clock so that every day 15 railcars loaded with 47.2 cubic metres of lumber were shipped out of town, a rate unmatched by any mill in Ontario.

lighting, a luxury then only available to the richest of individuals elsewhere, was directed into every home by generators located in the mill. Over time, Byng Inlet matured as merchants and other professionals took up residence, establishing businesses and hammering out the first vestiges of a real community. Within a few years, the community boasted a hotel (opened in 1899 by Joseph Legrow), a two-room school (School Section [SS] No. 1 Wallbridge, opened in 1897), a tiny one-doctor hospital, a bake house, and a blacksmith, in addition to the company store. The population stood at more than 600.

Despite its size, Byng Inlet remained isolated. The only practical link to the outside world was by steamer, while such roads that existed to and from town were little more than foot tracks impassable by wagon. During winter months, the frozen waters of Georgian Bay provided a more direct and less taxing alternative to the roads, and many people took advantage of it to visit Parry Sound. But it was a risky venture. More than one person perished when the cutter being ridden fell through the ice.

This state of remoteness ended when the Parry Sound–Sudbury branch of the Canadian Pacific Railway passed near Byng Inlet in 1908. The station was several kilometres inland, but for the first time an all-weather and affordable link to the outside world was available. It was common for residents to ride into Parry Sound on the morning train to shop and then return home on the evening train. The railway also provided an additional means by which the mill could ship lumber, the only one available year-round. Every day 15 railcars loaded with 47.2 cubic metres of lumber were shipped out of town, a rate unmatched by any mill in Ontario.

By the time the railway had come, the partnership of Holland and Emery had dissolved. For a time, Nelson Holland partnered with his cousin and the mill's former manager, Luther Graves, to form Holland and Graves. The final partnership to own the mill was Graves, Bigwood & Co., beginning December 31, 1906. Despite the name, Holland was still very much part of the mix; the main difference was that William E. Bigwood was brought in as the managing partner.

Jack Laird, who began working at the mill at age 12, earning $1 per day instead of the $1.75 paid to adults, spoke of his time there with Parry Sound historian John Macfie for the book *Parry Sound Logging Days*:

The largest sawmill ever to operate in Parry Sound District was the Graves, Bigwood & Co. operation at Byng Inlet. The company town at the mouth of the Magnetawan River was a booming home to hundreds of souls and amenities that included a dance hall and a silent movie theatre.

We worked eleven hours at night and ten in the daytime. The reason the night shift worked an extra hour was that they had a short shift on Saturday night. They got off three or four hours early on Sunday morning. You didn't get anything for nothing in those days. The eleven-hour shift got off at four o'clock Sunday morning so the mills wouldn't be running when the people were going to church. The mills were closed from four o'clock Sunday morning until six o'clock Monday morning.

The church Laird referred to was St. John the Divine Anglican Church, built in May 1909 on land leased by Graves, Bigwood & Co. "It is a church-ly, neat and comfortable building," reported the *Algoma Missionary News* in May 1909. "Mr. and Mrs. Bigwood and Mr. Braswell are very active in promoting the Church's cause. The prospects are full of hope." Three years

Among the first businesses to emerge in Byng Inlet was Joseph Legrow's hotel, which opened in 1898.

later, on August 25, 1912, the church was officially consecrated by Reverend George Thorneloe, the bishop of Algoma.

As the town grew and prospered, it became more metropolitan. Both a dance hall and a silent film movie house were built to entertain the locals, a stagecoach began operating between Byng Inlet and the railway station, and the shopping experience improved, with as many as five stores opening for business. The hotel expanded so it could accommodate 35 guests, and two additional boarding houses were built, largely for the use of seasonal employees. Baseball became a popular pastime, brought over by the numerous Americans employed at the mill. Games were played on a baseball diamond covered with sawdust. There was a sense of enthusiasm in the air that was almost tangible. Everyone was certain Byng Inlet was on the cusp of something great.

This buoyant mood was shattered on May 20, 1912. A stray spark from the steam plant started a fire that soon raged out of control, racing along floors, walls, and ceilings. Workers fought a desperate battle against the firestorm, but in the end were overwhelmed by the fury of the inferno. When at last the smoke cleared to allow the citizens of Byng Inlet to assess the extent of the damage, they were shocked to see only a charred scar where one of Canada's largest and most modern sawmills had stood only hours before. The destruction was complete. The mill itself was reduced to smoking cinders, but more importantly, the machinery was destroyed, as well. The fire had burned so hot that some of the machinery melted into unrecognizable slag.

For the second time in its existence, Byng Inlet faced an uncertain future. Would the mill, now owned by Graves, Bigwood & Co., be rebuilt? The livelihood of hundreds of people depended on it. In the end, the community was lucky. The company had yet to exhaust its timber rights along the Magnetawan watershed, so rebuild it would. Business returned to normal.

Graves, Bigwood & Co. was known as a particularly benevolent firm to work for, reflecting the personality of hands-on partner William Bigwood. Whereas most American lumbermen with operations in Ontario typically

A fire broke out on May 20, 1912, in Byng Inlet, beginning in the steam plant and reducing the sawmill to smoking cinders. The fire burned so hot that some of the machinery melted into unrecognizable slag. The damage was so extensive that it called into question Byng Inlet's future, since no one knew if Graves, Bigwood & Co. would rebuild the sawmill.

spent only such time there as necessary to keep their operations running, Bigwood was different. He devoted much of the year to living in Byng Inlet, a constant and reassuring presence, then returned to Toronto for the winter. He was popular among mill hands and their families, paying them fairly, conscious of their well-being, even engaging in baseball games and good-natured boxing matches with employees. Bigwood was described as "the best-loved man in the Canadian lumber trade."

But despite Bigwood's concerns for his employees' welfare, mills were an inherently dangerous place to work. Accidents, often gruesomely tragic, occurred with frightening regularity. James Riddle, for example, fell six metres from the elevated tramway into the river, where he struck his head on a floating log and drowned. Another time, the mill's broad saw — essentially a giant band saw — struck an unseen metal spike embedded in a log. The blade snapped and flailed about like the tentacles of a metallic octopus. The machine's operator, too slow to react, was beheaded. Merely living in Byng Inlet brought risks. A lack of communal sanitation and all drinking water being drawn from a single well meant outbreaks of typhoid were common.

A decade after the devastating fire of 1912, the mill suffered another blaze. When the first coils of smoke rose from the complex on August 15, 1922, residents immediately feared the worst. In the widespread devastation, would the mill be rebuilt this time? Would people be thrown out of work? The damage this time wasn't as extensive; it was largely confined to the planing mill and attached powerhouse. Both were total losses. So, too, were several boxcars of cut lumber ready to be shipped. Damages were estimated at $200,000. When the smoke cleared and the ashes cooled, repairs were made and the mill continued as before.

In truth, the end was nearer at hand than most citizens realized, or at least wanted to accept. Graves, Bigwood & Co. was felling trees at such a furious rate that only a decade later it began to feel the pinch of a nearly exhausted supply of pine. By the time William Bigwood died in 1927, the pine had finally run out, forcing the mill to close as Bigwood's company searched for new stands of timber to exploit. Most people in Byng Inlet followed, abandoning homes that no longer held any value or dreams. The town virtually disappeared overnight, with only a handful of loyalists remaining behind to keep the community's memory alive. It was the same sad yet entirely predictable demise suffered by dozens of other lumber towns across the province.

The community shrank so drastically that by 1931 the congregation of St. John the Divine stood at only 15; the final service was held in May of that year. A year later, as reported in the May edition of the *Algoma Missionary News*, the church was dismantled:

> One of the most beautiful of our churches, the Church of St. John the Divine at Byng Inlet, has been pulled down, much to our sorrow, the population having all moved away when the mill came to an end. It was a lovely little building, complete in every way, with full sets of vestments, hanging frontals, etc., and with several beautiful memorial windows.

The furnishings of the church were transferred to the Cowley Fathers of Bracebridge for use in their new chapel, while the bell currently resides in Trinity St. Albans Anglican Church in Bala, where a historic plaque tells how a bell from Georgian Bay ended up in Muskoka.

Today, while Byng Inlet may not be entirely lifeless, an almost deathly silence hangs over the faded town. Mere shadows of past glory are all that remain of the once-thriving mill community. Yet these shadows provide a powerful lure and remind us of Byng Inlet's rich past as one of Canada's largest sawmill towns.

Sawmill Lodge, a rustic cottage resort, occupies a waterfront location at what was the heart of historic Byng Inlet. The property's main building, the Lodge, dates to 1930 and was formerly a general store, replacing the original establishment that burned down on December 25, 1929. The hotel would have stood alongside it. Also on the expansive property are the impressive ruins of the mill. When walking in and around the stone foundations, imposing in their dimensions, the full extent of the operation becomes apparent. Only a fraction of the concrete foundations are visible — the remainder extends a distance into the forest and is obscured by overgrown bush — and yet the massiveness of the mill can be easily imagined as if it were still standing.

Lining the shores of Byng Inlet are rows of wooden pilings that slowly disappear into the waters. These crazily leaning posts once supported the extensive network of tramways and wharves by which lumber was shipped to hungry markets. A few old schooner slips remain, used by modern pleasure craft, while several original buildings provide a glimpse into the brief glory days of the community. These include the century-old school atop a granite hill just as one enters town; the former bakery, distinguishable by its unique stone construction; the one-time post office, now a private residence; and the odd home that formerly housed mill hands. A small cemetery huddles in the brush alongside Highway 645, just a few kilometres out of town. The headstones, cracked and tilting, represent the final resting place for men and women who lived and died, often under tragic circumstances, in Byng Inlet.

Tourism has restored some sense of vibrancy to the once-moribund community. The people who own the visiting boats and fishing craft tied to slips once occupied by schooners and scows swell the population of the little

The popularity of cottage living has seen Byng Inlet rebound in recent years, but remnants of the old community — the town of the sawmill era — are still evident. Among the more visible are the pilings driven into the bed of the bay, relics of the extensive wharf system that included tramways to deliver wood to waiting ships.

community on warm summer days. Byng Inlet will never again experience those heady times of a century ago when prosperity rested on a foundation of lumber and sawdust, but the remnants of that bygone era add character to it now. And the people of Byng Inlet? They're proud of their forebears who put the town on the map.

 To Get There

Take Highway 69 north from Parry Sound to Highway 529. From Highway 529, turn west on Highway 645. That takes you to, and ends, at Byng Inlet, among the vestiges of a once-thriving town and the frenzied industry that sustained it.

KIOSK

(Algonquin Park)

Algonquin Park is a protected wilderness reserve, and yet to the surprise of many, from the time it was created in 1893 vast tracts of its forests have been reserved for the exploitation of lumber companies. In fact, early Algonquin Park was filled with shanty camps and mills, as well as railway tracks that took felled trees to distant markets. There were even sizable villages that sprang up around frenetic mills.

The largest by far of these mill villages was Kiosk, a community that thrived for half a century in the park's northwest and came to an end not because the timber ran out but due to a political decision by the Ontario government. The sting of the loss is still felt by past residents.

Logging began in the forests of Algonquin well before the park was conceived. Logging for timber started about 1830, when James Wadsworth obtained a licence to cut red and white pine from Round Lake to the source of the Bonnechere River. Thousands of trees were felled each year; in 1846 alone, 141,600 cubic metres of red and white pine were harvested and floated down the Madawaska, Bonnechere, and Petawawa Rivers. Other loggers were given similar contracts to that granted to Wadsworth, among them William Mackey, the man responsible for kickstarting logging in what would become Algonquin Park's northwest, thus laying the foundation for Kiosk.

Eyeing vast tracts of untapped pine in the 1870s, Mackey purchased 777 square kilometres of timber rights adjoining the Amable du Fond River up to Lake Kioshkokwi and established logging camps along the waterways. It was a profitable trade, but the transport of logs from where they were felled to the mills where they were cut into lumber was an onerous undertaking. The only way to do it was to flush them down rivers — in Mackey's case the Mattawa and Ottawa — which took dozens of drivers and many months to complete.

The construction of the Canada Central Railway from Pembroke to Mattawa in 1881 helped shorten the river drives. In 1883, Mackey built a sawmill alongside the railway by Smith Lake; the village that grew around it was initially called Mackey's Mills in his honour but was later renamed Eau Claire Station.

In 1902, William Mackey sold the timber rights to lumber baron John Rudolphus Booth. He built a depot along the shores of Lake Kioshkokwi

Deep-woods camps from which loggers felled trees throughout the winter were established in the Kiosk area to provide the sawmill with the timber it required. In the early years, most of the loggers were Polish immigrants and seasoned lumbermen from Quebec, but the situation diversified as the years passed. Here we see a dormitory and cookery at one of the camps.

consisting of an office, a boarding house, a cookery, a store, and homes for as many as 60 individuals. Several satellite camps from which loggers felled trees throughout the winter were constructed, as well. Workers were mostly Polish immigrants and seasoned lumbermen from Quebec. Initially, supplies had to be shipped upriver from Eau Claire Station, but the situation improved considerably when the Canadian Northern Railway (CNoR), later incorporated into Canadian National Railways (CNR), was pushed through the northern extremity of Algonquin Park and past Booth's camp in 1915. Booth's backwoods community also grew at this time when the

Pictured here is a jack ladder drawing logs into the sawmill to be cut into lumber. Logs that had been cut all winter were driven down rivers by spring meltwater and collected in Lake Kioshkokwi. After being milled, the lumber was shipped to distant markets via train.

CNoR added several section buildings and a handful of staff to what already existed.

J.R. Booth died in 1925, and within a few years, his heirs closed shop on Lake Kioshkokwi. Only the CNoR buildings remained inhabited and in use, but that didn't spell the end of Booth's community — far from it. Before long, it swelled into Algonquin's largest community, thanks to the vision and enterprise of Sydney Staniforth.

Sydney Staniforth was a career lumberman. Employed by the Fassett Lumber Company of Quebec, he served as managing director of its operation at Fossmill, 18 kilometres west of Booth's depot at Lake Kioshkokwi. When the mill at Fossmill burned down in 1934, the once-thriving company was already on its last shaky legs, and Staniforth couldn't convince the ownership to rebuild it. But Staniforth knew there were still profits to be made from lumbering in the region. While most of the pine was exhausted, there was still plenty of hardwood timber available for harvesting. In 1935, Staniforth made a deal with J.R. Booth's heirs to buy the timber rights

Career lumberman Sydney Staniforth purchased the J.R. Booth timber rights in Algonquin Park in 1935 and formed the Staniforth Lumber Company. In a real coup, Staniforth received permission from the Ontario government to build a sawmill within the confines of the park.

Booth had purchased in 1902. A year later he formed the Staniforth Lumber Company. In a real coup, Staniforth received permission from the Ontario government — desperate to get men to work during the dark days of the Great Depression — to build a sawmill within the confines of Algonquin Park.

Staniforth centred his operation on the site of the previous Booth camp. The mill was erected on the shores of Lake Kioshkokwi at the mouth of the Amable du Fond River, while satellite camps to supply the mill with timber were established deep in the forest. Most of the workers were former employees of the Fossmill outfit who had been thrown into unemployment by the fire. Many still resided in Fossmill. They worked a six-day week and then returned to their families in Fossmill, walking the 23 kilometres or hitching a ride on a train to their homes. Monday through Friday, they were housed alongside permanent residents in the old Booth bunkhouse or in one of the handful of pre-existing cabins.

Within a few short years, Staniforth's nascent community was granted a post office. Lake Kioshkokwi was deemed too long and unwieldy for a name, so it was shortened to Kiosk. Staniforth's bush village now had a name.

Two townsites were laid out, one on either side of the Amable du Fond River. By 1941, Kiosk had matured into a true village, with a company store, perhaps a dozen newly built residences, and a population of 100. The mill was enlarged significantly and expanded to add a dry kiln and planing mill.

Growth continued unabated. A decade later, Kiosk boasted a large wooden Catholic church, a school, a recreation hall, a baseball diamond, and an outdoor skating rink. The mill was augmented again so that it now had a veneer plant. A small plant on the Amable du Fond River supplied every household with water and electricity. The population now stood at 186 permanent residents. Soon enough, it topped 300. At the same time, the sense of isolation under which residents lived began to lift as a modern, all-season road was opened from Kiosk to Highway 17.

Kiosk was a company town through and through, which had its drawbacks. The only shopping option was Staniforth's store, though in fairness prices were reasonable and stock extensive. Worse, at least as far as the workers were concerned, was the fact that Kiosk was technically a dry town,

The Staniforth mill was a massive complex that included a dry kiln, a planing mill, and a veneer plant. More than 250 men and women were employed there.

meaning liquor was prohibited. Residents might have found a way around the designation, but they had to do so cautiously, since their livelihoods hung in the balance.

Even as business thrived and the population mushroomed through the 1940s and 1950s, Kiosk experienced its share of strife. There was labour discontent, leading to the formation of a union in 1950. Almost immediately thereafter, workers demanding better wages and working conditions went on strike. Another strike followed in 1955. Then, in 1958, Kiosk's visionary founder, Sydney Staniforth, died in a car accident, age 73. The community mourned the loss of its benefactor and prayed that his three sons — Harold, Donald, and Robert — would run the company as wisely as he had.

They needn't have worried. The 1960s represented the apogee for company and town. By the end of the decade, Kiosk was home to 600 people, 250 of them employed at the mill, and there were now 80 buildings on the townsite. A handsome new brick school with three classrooms was built, while the original school was repurposed as a community centre. Ownership

Religion was very important to Kiosk's francophone residents. The community boasted a large wooden Roman Catholic church.

loosened its rules, allowing competing retailers to open — there were now three — and alcohol was no longer forbidden.

But then, in 1969, Kiosk's future suddenly became cloudy. The Staniforth lease expired, and the Ontario government, uncertain that a residential community and mill were appropriate for a provincial park, refused to renew the lease for anything more than a year at a time. Two years later, the Staniforth brothers decided to sell. Their attention was diverted elsewhere by new timber rights in Quebec, and besides, there were rumblings that the Ontario government might soon cancel their Kiosk lease for good. Driven by concern for Kiosk's long-term viability, the Staniforths sold the mill to Universal Oil Products but agreed to remain on as advisers. Suddenly, after decades of prosperity, Kiosk faced uncertainty.

Then, on July 13, 1973, the village's fate was decided. At around 11:30 p.m. that day, the tranquility of the hot summer evening was shattered by alarms and cries of panic. The mill was on fire, the flames reaching hundreds of metres into the sky and moving too fast for the inferno to be contained. Townsfolk gathered to watch the mill be consumed over the next 90 minutes. It was, some thought darkly, like a funeral pyre for the community itself. And they were proven right.

During the months that followed, Kiosk's residents lived in a state of perpetual anxiety, their lives and futures in suspension. Would the mill be rebuilt? If so, when? If not, what would become of them? The people of Kiosk were in a bind because while they owned their homes, they didn't own the land — the park belonged to the Crown and couldn't be sold. Everyone, understandably, worried about what the future held.

Their worst fears were realized the following year, when the provincial government unveiled its master plan for Algonquin Park, a response to the rising controversy about logging there. The 1974 plan zoned the park into areas that allowed logging and others that didn't, set out specific strategies for the conduct of forest management activities, and transferred the timber licences previously held by 20 companies to the newly established Algonquin Forestry Authority (AFA), a commercially oriented Crown agency that henceforth was responsible for all logging operations in the park.

The plan not only didn't include rebuilding the Kiosk mill but also signalled that the Ontario government had the community in its sights, as well. Residents were told they would have to leave in what was essentially an eviction notice. The Kiosk Community Association campaigned hard, putting forward several possible compromises. It was hoped, for example, since Kiosk was just three kilometres inside the park, that boundaries could be redrawn ever so slightly to allow people to purchase their homes and the community to continue. In the end, there was no budging the government from its position. Residents had to vacate by 1996. Compensation for the loss of their homes was offered, but the longer residents remained, the less they would receive.

Many people resisted relocation at first, driven by stubborn determination. They held on to their homes and memories with an iron grip. Slowly but surely, an exodus that began as a trickle turned into a mass migration. By the close of the 1970s, the population had contracted from more than 600 to around 150. The school and post office closed in the early 1980s, and by 1986, the population was reduced to fewer than 100 as even the most stubborn gave up. The final diehards were gone by 1992. Some families took the compensation, but others refused to allow their homes to be bulldozed and removed them to off-park properties.

For several years, the townsite remained in stasis — much of it still in existence but hollow and lifeless. As a child, Amber Valade visited Kiosk with her mother, who had grown up in the shadow of the mill. It was her mother's way of keeping the memory of Kiosk alive. The experience touched Amber. "You could feel the sadness in the empty homes," she remembered. "It was a true ghost town. There were still probably 10 houses remaining when I was there, and you could see the yards where homes had stood before being torn down. It was truly sad."

Today, no original building remains; the Ministry of Natural Resources and Forestry was extremely thorough in razing the village. The site is now a camping ground and canoe access point for backwoods excursions into the depths of Algonquin Park. The park permit office occupies the site of the old Booth bunkhouse, but few campers have any idea that where they pitch their tents was once the location of a sprawling mill complex, or that the dirt pathways they follow through the woods were village streets not so long ago.

While the Ontario Ministry of Natural Resources and Forestry razed Kiosk to the ground, it wasn't nearly so thorough with the deep-woods logging camps. They were left to rot slowly away, so atmospheric ruins remained until recently.

Generally, few visitors have any idea there was once a thriving community here until they stumble upon building foundations amid the trees. To find Kiosk's sole remaining structure, one has to go farther afield. In order to save the church from destruction, it was removed from the townsite to a farm just outside the park's boundaries. However, the CNoR line upon which the mill depended for its very existence is no longer in use.

Although Kiosk is gone, logging continues in the park, employing forest management techniques to ensure ecological integrity, forest diversity, and sustainability. While 50 percent of the park is available for logging, harvesting activities only take place on approximately 1 percent of the forested area each year. Less than 5 percent of felling takes the form of clear-cutting, and that's only done in areas where the dominant tree species — poplar, white birch, red and jack pine, for example — require open sunlight conditions to germinate and grow new seedlings. Harvested wood is shipped to one of 20 mills located in communities adjacent to the park, continuing to employ 3,000 people and supporting rural economies.

Kiosk was the last lumber community to exist within the boundaries of Algonquin Park. Those who fought to stave off its demise might as well have tried to stop the sun from rising and setting. But its death is sad, nonetheless. So, too, is the fact that so little remains to remind us of the village's rich history.

To Get There

Kiosk is located in Algonquin Park's extreme northwest. From Highway 17, take Highway 630 south. The road passes through some stunning landscape before terminating at the Kiosk Campground. Remember that while this might be one of Algonquin Park's nearly 30 access points, facilities here are limited to a campground office — campsites can be booked up to five months in advance and often sell out — and there's no cellphone reception. A visit to the Algonquin Logging Museum (algonquinpark.on.ca/visit/locations /algonquin-logging-museum.php) is instructive, since it brings to life the story of logging in the park from the early square timber days of the 1830s to modern forestry management as conducted by the Algonquin Forestry Authority. The museum consists of both a log reception building and a 1.3-kilometre trail that leads visitors past relics and reproductions from the logging past: a recreated camboose shanty, log chutes, squared timbers, old stables, a blacksmith shop, sleighs for transporting logs, and a steam-powered "alligator" (a tug that could portage across land between lakes and river). The Algonquin Logging Museum is located just inside Algonquin Park's East Gate on Highway 60.

DESAULNIERS

(West Nipissing, Nipissing District)

Desaulniers is a one-time farming community in Nipissing District whose rail-side buildings, fields dotted with hay crofts, and bustling main street have virtually vanished with the passage of time. In the late 19th century, a number of francophone communities were established in the relatively fertile soils north of Lake Nipissing. Settlement was encouraged by Catholic priests who saw increasing the French-Canadian population in the region as a means to boost the fortunes of the Roman Catholic Church there.

The foremost proponent of this settlement was Father Charles-Alfred Paradis, who devoted his energies to colonizing the area between Lake Nipissing and Temagami with francophone settlers — some from northern Michigan, a good many from Quebec — and establishing new parishes. But while Paradis gets most of the credit for this wave of successful settlement, he couldn't claim it for Desaulniers. Instead, the village was the product of the tireless encouragement and campaigning of Father A.L. Desaulniers.

Some sources claim Desaulniers was a rival of Paradis. What is certain is that he was cut from an entirely different cloth. Whereas Paradis was larger than life, a man who seemed to enjoy the spotlight and ruffling feathers — he once ran afoul of both secular and religious leadership by opposing the logging practices that formed the foundation of the region's economy and was essentially exiled to the United States for a time — Father Desaulniers was more conventional and circumspect. While they differed in personality and approach, the two clergymen shared a similar vision of establishing French colonies in the Nipissing region.

In the early 1890s, Father Desaulniers began campaigning for settlement in Gibbons Township. There were already a few homesteaders in the region — the first may have been the Serre family — but with the priest's encouragement a wave of eager settlers arrived between 1893 and 1895, hoping to cash in on the promise of personal self-sufficiency Father Desaulniers was promoting. They built homes and cleared land for farms. Charles Joanis opened a store that same year, and the following spring, on April 1, 1896, was granted a post office licence. Joseph Courchesne stepped forward to erect a sawmill to provide settlers with lumber and shingles for homes and barns. The young community, desperately fighting to establish roots in the Northern Ontario soil, was named Desaulniers for the visionary priest.

Among these land-hungry settlers were Misael Bigras and his wife, Philomène, who ventured west from Quebec in the late 1890s for a fresh start. Right up until her death in 1930, Philomène, who was Métis, reminded her children, and their children, of the rich legacy of the family dating back 350 years.

The story of the Bigrases wasn't that different from those of the many others who staked futures on Desaulniers. Regardless of one's background and lineage, though, settling Desaulniers was a difficult life at first, and many must have wondered if the village did indeed have God's blessing. Homesteaders struggled throughout the summer to clear their land and cultivate enough crops to feed their families. Potatoes were the undisputed staple crop of early Desaulniers because they could be grown successfully and with comparatively little maintenance, even in the less-than-ideal soil of the Canadian Shield. Yield per acre was greater than any other crop, so

Among Desaulniers's earliest settlers were Misael Bigras and his Métis wife, Philomène. Their son, Elijah — pictured here with his wife, Mathilda, and their infant son, Albert, in 1909 — took over the family farm and ran it well into the 20th century.

Trains haven't passed through Desaulniers in generations. The rail station is long gone, the only reminder being the concrete foundation of the water tower. The rails have long since been lifted. The former right-of-way is now a recreational trail.

potatoes became a prominent part of the diet. Naturally, other vegetables were also planted, grains sown, and livestock — principally sows and chickens — reared for a more balanced diet.

After bringing in harvests in the fall and putting their farms to bed for the year, most men then sought employment in lumber camps for the duration of the winter. Even with this additional income, many families found it difficult to break even in the best of years. But they persevered.

However, the situation changed dramatically in 1913 with the decision by Canadian Northern Railway (later part of Canadian National Railways or CNR) to lay tracks northward through the bush beyond Lake Nipissing and pass through Desaulniers. The railway established a sizable station and siding, a residence for the agent in charge, homes for section workers whose job it was to maintain the tracks, and a boarding house for overnight guests. Towering over them all was a water tower to supply the steam engines that passed through multiple times per day.

The railway provided a welcome boost of prosperity for the small farming community, transforming it seemingly overnight. Now that there was a means

Farms kept sizable dairy herds to sell milk to a local cheese factory. Cows required winter fodder, so haying was an important task. Here, 19-year-old Oliva Quenneville uses a mechanical rake to cut hay. Oliva was one of 15 children fathered by Wilfred Quenneville.

for produce to be shipped to distant markets, entrepreneurs stepped forward to profit by it. No sooner had the tracks passed through than Lionel Vallières opened a cheese factory. Area farmers rejoiced. Many struggled to make ends meet raising crops in the northern soil, but now here was the answer to their prayers — supplying Vallières with milk represented a new source of income. Many farmers subsequently invested in expanding dairy herds and did well, and new settlers arrived in the area to take up hoe and plough.

In 1915, it was announced that Lampert Bros. Lumber of Minnesota, which had an expansive timber line along the Sturgeon River, was looking for a site in the region to build a sawmill. Residents of Desaulniers rejoiced when the company ultimately located the mill in their community. Four hectares of land a mere stone's throw from the railway station were purchased from A.B. Serre. The steam-powered mill was situated along a creek running through a gulley. Cut lumber was loaded aboard wagons and driven up the hill to the railway siding, then piled onto flatcars for shipment to the chain of yards owned by Lampert Bros. in the U.S. Midwest. The mill provided another welcome source of employment for many local men.

Although Desaulniers was primarily an agricultural community, a sawmill owned by Lampert Bros. Lumber of Minnesota provided welcome employment for many. The gully in which the mill operated is, ironically, completely wooded over today.

Suddenly, virtually overnight, Desaulniers' fortunes were reversed, and worn-down homesteaders began to bask in relative prosperity, which led to further growth. At one time, Desaulniers had a population larger than nearby Field. Two schools — one public, the other a French separate school — saw to educating the village's youth. A boarding house sprung up beside the railway station, offering modest but nonetheless welcome overnight accommodation. Then a second store opened. These were good times.

Incredibly, especially in light of the religious auspices under which the community was founded, it was more than two decades after Desaulniers was founded before a church was built to see to the spiritual needs of the devout Catholics who overwhelmingly made up the community. And even then it wasn't without controversy.

When talk of a church first surfaced, it was resisted by David Joseph Scollard, the bishop of Sault Ste. Marie Diocese, in which Desaulniers was located. Scollard, a 53-year-old cleric of Irish descent, didn't care for French-Canadian migration that threatened to alter the demographic balance of the Nipissing region. He had made consistent efforts to deter French-Canadian inroads since being named bishop in 1904, though with varying degrees of success. Moreover, years later, he was apparently angry that French

Two schools, one public, the other a French separate school, educated area youth. This class photo (1924–25) is likely from the public school.

Canadians were lukewarm about serving in the Canadian military when it was engaged in the First World War; voluntary enlistment in Quebec lagged far behind the rest of Canada. The bishop's opposition to francophone colonization of his diocese was so entrenched that it put a halt to any new settlement schemes.

Scollard was cold toward the idea of a church in Desaulniers. When, on March 18, 1915, residents sent him a petition imploring him to change his mind, Scollard penned a response that was equal parts incredulous and vindictive. "I must tell you I am surprised at the large number of names on this petition," he wrote. "The majority would appear to be in favour of a parish church at Desaulniers and the priests' residence in that place also. It would be good to see also who signed the enclosed petition to find out if they knew what they were signing. I am certainly surprised to see 72 names on that petition." Scollard continued to drag his heels.

Fed up with official intransigence, residents moved ahead on their own. Construction of a church started later that year. The wooden church that emerged was large and well appointed, with a confessional, a beautifully designed altar, a bell in the steeple, and a statue of the church's patron, St. Anne. It aptly reflected the congregation's devotion. Residents were, with good reason, proud of what they had built.

Not everyone was impressed, however. Scollard raged and adamantly refused to recognize the new church. He claimed that since he hadn't been consulted on its construction, the church had no official sanction and he had no obligation to recognize it. Scollard apparently said something to the effect of "this church was built without my permission and as long as I have one eye open this building will never become a church." After hearing this, residents of Desaulniers apparently "prayed for both of his eyes to close, and real soon," a decidedly unchristian sentiment but reflective of the depth of the hurt felt by the congregation.

Over the next year, pressure on Scollard intensified. Residents of Desaulniers wouldn't take no for an answer and continued to pester the bishop. Many local priests backed them and urged Scollard to reconsider his position. Finally, facing a challenge to his authority, Scollard relented — in a fashion. On September 16, 1916, he officially opened St. Anne's. But in a pique of pettiness, he still refused to consecrate it. Nonetheless, and despite mutual bitterness, the people of Desaulniers at last had their church. The first mass was held on September 25, presided over by Father C.P. Thériault of Field. A year later, on July 29, 1917, a benediction ceremony was held for the statue of St. Anne.

Scollard remained unmoved in his decision to withhold consecration. In fact, his views only hardened as the years passed and he aged. The bishop held this grudge and withheld consecration until his death in 1934. As a result of his vindictiveness, Desaulniers' house of worship, impressive as it might have been, was technically never an official Catholic church. St. Anne's became known as "The Church That Never Was."

By the time Scollard died, Desaulniers was in decline. Times were changing. The cheese factory was long gone, and the sawmill had ceased operation. The train station and related facilities were shut down, and CNR employees transferred elsewhere. Several farming families had moved away in search of employment in larger centres such as Sturgeon Falls or North Bay. It wasn't long before the church no longer hosted masses, its pews empty.

The residents weathered the downturn in fortunes and stayed on. Desaulniers remained a small but thriving farming community throughout the 1940s. In fact, the village was doing well enough that travelling salesman Wilfred Philippe, a man with a keen eye for a good business deal, decided to purchase the general store from retiring Albemi St. Louis in 1947. In fairness, Philippe had another motivation — while visiting his sister, Yvonne Bigras, he'd fallen in love with a local woman named Denise Trepanier. He no longer had itchy feet; now Wilfred wanted to settle down and run a store, which seemed like the perfect fit for his skill set and personality. With business still doing well, Philippe saw fit to greatly expand the store to include hardware supplies, a large shed for feed and seed, and gas pumps out front. The store was also home to the village's only telephone.

St. Anne's Church had always been a focal point of the community, so when it was closed, the general store became more important to the social fabric of Desaulniers than ever before. People came there to pick up mail, make purchases, or place telephone calls, lingering by the pot-bellied stove or on the wide veranda to catch up on gossip and share news with neighbours.

While lumbering brought Desaulniers prosperity, the community's foundation was built on farming. It was always a race against nature to bring in the harvest, so multiple generations of a family often shared labour, as seen here.

Wilfred and Denise sold the store to a local co-op in 1951, the beginning of a sad decade as Desaulniers floundered. The church, long since abandoned and increasingly ramshackle with neglect, was torn down and its lumber sold. Farms, the foundation of the community, were abandoned. They had never quite thrived as Father Desaulniers had promised, and second or third generations had given up on the dreams of their parents and grandparents. The post office shut down on June 30, 1960, and the general store itself followed suit a few years later.

When the sign on the general store turned to CLOSED permanently, it marked the end of Desaulniers as a distinct community. People still lived in the area, naturally, and some continued to farm as their ancestors had before them, but everything that had made the village distinct — church, schools, businesses, train station — was all gone. By that time, fewer than 50 people called Desaulniers home.

Over the next few decades, the community receded further into the mists of time as farms reverted to pasture and town lots weeded over. Road realignments claimed some of the village. Abandoned homes and barns collapsed under the weight of age and winter snow loads, often slowly, reluctantly, as if unwilling to accept that the village was no more.

Desaulniers is fairly silent now and largely unrecognizable as a community where trains hissed to a stop in a cloak of steam and from which lumber by the railcar was shipped. Today, the village's one-time main street looks like nothing more than a country laneway, with the store, railway station, station master's home, and water tower having long vanished, though the foundations of the last can still be found if one knows where to look. The ravine where the mill once nestled is now completely wooded over.

A few period homes remain occupied. The weathered boarding house is slowly sinking into the ground. Eventually, it, too, will collapse. Even the railway tracks have been removed. The former railbed is now a multi-use recreational trail that extends off into the distance as if reaching to the distant past when Desaulniers was a thriving community.

Desaulniers's sole remaining commercial structure is the one-time boarding house, formerly frequented by rail travellers and men employed at the sawmill.

To Get There

Follow Highway 64 north from Highway 17 at Sturgeon Falls to Field, then west on Highway 539 for seven kilometres to Desaulniers Road. The boarding house is right before the one-time railway right-of-way.

13

MILBERTA

(Kerns Township, Temiskaming District)

Ontario's north is dominated by the rock of the Canadian Shield, which proved largely inarable despite numerous attempts to plant farms atop it. But there's an island of arable land just northwest of Lake Temiskaming — the Little Claybelt, which runs from Englehart down the Wabi River to Lake Temiskaming (a larger claybelt exists even farther north in Cochrane District). Anywhere fertile land was found it was inevitable settlement would follow.

In due course, communities sprang up in the Little Claybelt. Among them was Kerns Township's Milberta. Whereas most of these places were flyspeck hamlets, Milberta developed into a sizable community with a distinct core — a true village. But it wasn't an easy path from bush farm to thriving village.

The initial tentative steps to settle Kerns Township took place in 1897. Samuel Hogg and John Newton both registered lands that year, but Hogg gets credit for being the community's first resident because he was first off the mark to build a home. Regardless of who was first, both men left their marks on Milberta.

Milberta sits within the geological anomaly that is the Little Claybelt, a narrow band of arable soil nestled in the Canadian Shield. The forests were cleared and gave way to vast golden fields of grain waving in the wind. Although Milberta faded, the Little Claybelt continues to support numerous farms today.

Born in Northumberland County, Ontario, on February 20, 1872, Samuel Hogg was the 10th of 11 children and experienced trials early in life. He was only 12 years old when his father died, casting the family's future in doubt. Growing up quickly, the youngster left school and apprenticed as a blacksmith under his brother George, nine years his senior. Hogg was 25 when he ventured north to Temiskaming District in May 1897, built a log home, and established a farm. It seems likely that the move was made in anticipation of his pending wedding to Alberta Rachael Mitchel. They would need a home and a means to support themselves, after all, and opportunities for men like Hogg were hard to come by in Northumberland County. Perhaps Alberta's father even made the wedding contingent on the young man possessing the income to take care of a wife.

Samuel and Alberta were wed and moved north the following year. The couple farmed with some success, but that wasn't enough for Samuel. In the next few years, he also opened a blacksmith shop and a sawmill to cater to the other settlers taking up land in the vicinity. In 1901, Hogg was successful in his petition to be named postmaster. As such, the honour of christening the community fell to him. He came up with Milberta: *Mil* because he owned a sawmill, and *berta* in honour of his beloved wife, Alberta. He served as postmaster for only three years, but it was long enough to cement his legacy.

Following Hogg as postmaster was John Newton, the same man who narrowly lost the race to be Milberta's first settler. John Newton and his family arrived in Kerns Township almost simultaneously with Samuel Hogg to register the north half of a lot in Concession 2 on what would be the east side of Milberta. John was born and spent the first five decades of his life on a bucolic farm in Cobourg, Ontario, and it was there in relative comfort that he and his wife, Ellen, raised their children. What compelled John, age almost 50, to uproot his family from their well-established lives and head to the unsettled Temiskaming District in 1897? Was it the challenge? Was he seduced by the glowing words of newspapers and promoters? We'll likely never know, but regardless of the reason, he set himself the task of taming the bush.

John Newton established a farm and a boarding house where practically all the early settlers stayed while building their own cabins. Ellen was a great comfort for the women arriving in the region, "a mother to many of the homesick brides who came to the brush country to make their homes." In 1904, Newton took over the position of postmaster, holding it for three years before handing it over for two more years to son John Junior, who often went by his middle name, Thomas, to avoid confusion with his father.

Other settlers followed on the heels of Hogg and Newton, including the Free, Irving, Jibb, Parcells, Penelton, Philips, Thompson, and Travail families. Their backgrounds were disparate, their origins varied, but all shared the same hardships, and years later would reflect on them with an odd mixture of pride and grim humour. "When we think or talk of these old times," wrote Mrs. Dan Jarvis in an undated note published in the *Temiskaming Women's Institute*, "with their hardships, freezing in winter, and being tortured by mosquitoes and flies of all sorts in the summer, greasy with fly oil, black from charred logs when logging, and tired with long toil, we do it with a queer feeling of something akin to love trickling around in our heart."

The settlement was still in its infancy, barely standing on uncertain legs, when it was very nearly destroyed. In July 1901, a raging forest fire rose from the west and swept across Kerns, Hudson, and Dymond Townships. "Every stump in the clearing was on fire, and the roots and muck in the ground were continuously spreading the fire," wrote Alberta Hogg in a letter preserved in *Milberta Tweedsmuir History*. "The wind was terrific, and it was indeed a hard struggle to protect home the pile of lumber so dearly made. The fire would come through in steps, each step being like a new fire. One could hear the roar of the fire coming before it would reach the clearing and I cannot express the terror of it."

Things were so dire that at one point it looked as if the fire would overwhelm the Hoggs. Samuel prepared a platform to be put halfway down the well in the hope that it would shelter his wife and young child. As for himself, he prepared for the worst. Thankfully, the winds shifted at the last minute and the fire swept in a new direction, sparing his family. "We did not need to go down that well, which was perhaps fortunate," Alberta wrote, "as in later fires, several people who sought this means of escape, were suffocated."

Desperate homesteaders fought the fire and feared for their lives for a week until rains finally came and doused the flames. The devastation was heart-rending. Newly built homes and barns were razed, crops were reduced to ashes that blew away on the summer wind, and valuable timber in the forests was destroyed. Hogg lost his sawmill, and both the store that settlers depended on for supplies and the school — built just the year prior — were consumed.

And yet the people of Milberta weren't deterred. Indeed, they even found silver linings in the devastation. Alberta Hogg remembered that "the fire benefited us as the brush and lighter timber was burned, making it easier to clear the farms."

Rebuilding began immediately as burnt homes and barns were rapidly replaced and Hogg rebuilt his sawmill. The land was surveyed and town lots were laid out. Religion was front of mind for these settlers, and a Presbyterian congregation started to take shape. Hogg, who by now was reeve of the newly opened Kerns Township, donated land and lumber for a church and

Samuel Hogg, who named Milberta, donated the land and lumber for the Presbyterian (now United) church. His wife, Milberta, was the organist. Built in 1902, the church survived the great fire of 1922, the Depression, and Milberta's decline, but its future is sadly now in doubt.

was also the primary carpenter in its construction. However, the Hogg contribution didn't end there. When the church was launched in 1902, Alberta Hogg acted as the organist. A Baptist church opened in Milberta around the same time, and the nearby hamlet known as the Highland Settlement, only a few kilometres distance east, raised a Methodist church.

Milberta grew slowly but steadily. A reporter from the *Newmarket Era* visited in October 1903, and according to the story he filed for October 9, he found "three stores in Milberta, sawmill, Presbyterian church, and about a dozen houses." While still just a flyspeck frontier hamlet, settlers were apparently bullish on the future that lay ahead for Milberta. The *Newmarket Era* reporter interviewed John Newton, who said that "he would not exchange his holdings today for 200 acres in his old neighbourhood."

In his report, the *Newmarket Era* scribe somehow neglected to mention that Milberta also boasted a school. In 1899, with the population increasing,

Pictured here is Milberta School Section (SS) No. 1A Kerns, class of 1916. The school was opened in 1900 but razed by a forest fire a year later. Rebuilt, the school endured for six decades before closing for good in 1961.

trustees were selected to establish a school. Samuel Hogg and John Newton, true to character, stepped forward to serve as trustees. Newton offered a parcel of land, and Hogg again donated lumber from his sawmill. School Section (SS) No. 1A Kerns Township, the first of what would eventually be four schools in Kerns, was built in the summer of 1900 and opened to a class of about a dozen children. The community was understandably proud. But elation turned to despair a year later when, in July 1901, a raging wildfire swept over the school and reduced it to cinders. Rallying, with Hogg once more supplying lumber, the school was rebuilt with great haste so that it was ready for classes in September.

Within a few more years, Milberta boasted a couple of grocery stores, a hardware store, and a butcher shop, and Thomas Newton opened a short-lived hotel. A women's institute was founded in 1906, and Milberta athletes played in a softball league that included teams from Uno Park and Thornloe.

A journalist from the *Daily British Whig* toured the region in the autumn of 1914 and published a story on October 23. He was clearly impressed with

Crews are shown here building Milberta Road in 1902. When Milberta was established in the mid-1890s, there was no road access. The only link between the community and the outside world was via the Wabi River, which flows into Lake Temiskaming at New Liskeard. One look at this photo and it's easy to see why it took seven years for a road to be built through such challenging terrain.

what he found. "The new settlers had been in for ten to fifteen years and already in many cases had large clearings and good buildings equal to their requirements," he wrote. "I saw fields cleared of stumps, fenced with wire or timbers; crops in good condition; in some cases, fairly heavy stocks of cattle and horses; besides everything to make their families comfortable, and many stretches of good roads, with churches and good schools convenient."

Clearly impressed, the journalist continued to paint the picture of a flourishing agricultural centre. "Take an example: an old acquaintance of mine from Oxford County had located near Milberta eight years before with quite a family, including two stalwart sons. In that time, they had cleared up 90 acres, fenced it with wire, built a frame house worth $1,500 and a new bank barn, 40 x 88 feet, which he said was none too large for his crop. He had a good head of cattle and several fine horses, and plenty of water and wood."

Based on this glowing description, one would think Milberta was on the cusp of something great, that residents could look to the future with confidence and ambition. Sadly, that wasn't to be the case.

The summer and early autumn of 1922 were unusually dry, leaving the forests and fields little more than kindling. The conditions were perfect for what began as a small wildfire to explode into catastrophe. October 2, 1922, started off like any other day, but by mid-morning the sky was blackened with smoke, blotting out the sun and throwing the landscape into eerie shadow. Soon, raging flames raced across Temiskaming District, incinerating 1,680 square kilometres. Milberta was directly in the path of the inferno, and there was little anyone could do except flee as the conflagration approached.

The fires were extinguished when the winds abated and rain and snow began to fall on October 5. The loss was staggering. Thousands were left homeless, and 43 lives were lost. Some communities — North Cobalt, Haileybury, Thornloe, and Heaslip — were wiped from the map. For its part, Milberta still stood but was badly scarred. Many homes and barns were burnt to the ground, their inhabitants — people and livestock — cast into the elements. Some lost everything they owned. And then a fresh hell descended upon the stunned village: temperatures dropped precipitously, but there were few buildings to seek shelter in and little wood to burn for warmth. A long winter lay ahead.

Some chose to rebuild, others gave up. The fortitude of those who elected to endure was tested further by two successive autumns — 1927 and 1928 — of killing frost and destructive weather. A despondent farm wife was moved to pen a letter to members of women's institutes, begging for assistance:

> May I point out to you that whatever relief can be sent to us should come, to be effective, as soon as possible. This has been a hard fall, and if clothing could be sent now before the very cold weather comes, it would be much appreciated. We had fifteen acres of as fine fall wheat as could grow and only saved it fit for feed. It would not thresh. We lost all our

spring crop. This is the second year. In the meantime, if the branches in old Ontario could help us with warm clothing for our children, it would be a step in the right direction.

One can almost hear the desperation in her words. More farmers threw in the towel after this setback, knowing they could make more money in mining or lumbering.

Herbert Jibb was one of those farmers who persisted and indeed thrived. As a teenager in 1900, Herbert and several of his brothers ventured north from Northumberland County to search for work. They took a train as far as Temiskaming Station, boarded the steamship *Meteor* to New Liskeard, then walked 19 kilometres over primitive roads to spend the winter cutting trees in a logging camp. Herbert must have liked what he saw, because after meeting Victoria Louise Gertrude May in 1909, he brought her farther north to take up farming in Milberta.

Herbert and Victoria had a bountiful marriage. They raised nine children together, boasted a large herd of horses that was the envy of the region,

Herbert and Victoria Jibb accumulated 13 farms in Kerns Township, the one in this photo among them. Each of their eight sons was given a farm as a wedding gift. Still farming to the very end, Herbert died in a tractor accident on November 10, 1949.

and amassed 13 farms across Kerns Township. When each of their eight sons married, he was given a farm as a wedding gift. Herbert was still farming to the very end. He died in a tractor accident on November 10, 1949, still doing what he loved most.

While the Jibbs were amassing farms, Milberta's fortunes continued to decline. By the 1940s, there was little to recommend the village. A scant handful of farms and homes remained, but the core of the community was gone. The sidewalk made of boards that ran along the roadside was still there, but it led nowhere as the businesses disappeared.

Dan Jarvis was born in Milberta in 1934, and childhood recollections shared in 2020 with the Little Claybelt Homesteaders Museum speak of a fading community. "There had been a Baptist church down by the school," he told the museum, "but all that was left was a hole in the ground when I was a kid. In front of it were chokecherry trees and we used to pick them. I watched the Newtons' house [by then empty] burn down around 1939–40. Beside it had once stood a store. I remember it as a hole in the ground, full of junk."

A view looking north on main street (Milberta Road) in 1917. The church is at left. Opposite is a string of homes and businesses linked by a wooden sidewalk that ran all the way to Concession 3. Edson Jibb, a brother of Herbert Jibb, sits in his car, one of the first automobiles residents would have seen.

The Hogg blacksmith shop had also become a junkyard, Jarvis recalled, the aging building surrounded by a tangle of rusting and wrecked automobiles. And another of the former shops was being used by Jarvis's farming father for storage. The post office, then under Herbert Tice, closed on March 31, 1942.

Despite the atrophy all around it, the school remained very much in use. Jarvis received his education there, and it remains preserved like a photograph in his mind. "Inside the school we were seated wherever we fit," he remembered. "There were about 30 kids, and the one room was pretty well full. One of the students, Jim Willard, was in charge of the fire [in the wood stove]. He was around my age. Usually, the fire in the winter would burn most of the night until it burned out. The school room was really cold. There was a big bank of windows on the north side of the building. The school sat on a hill and there was nothing to stop the wind. We had to pull our desks up around the box stove to keep warm. We burned all the fronts of the desks doing that."

Jarvis had scattered and incomplete memories of teachers and lessons, but perhaps not unsurprisingly, the joy of playing with schoolmates remained vividly etched in his mind despite the passage of eight decades. "For recess at school, we had a ball field by the Presbyterian church grounds," he told the museum. "In the winter, we skated and played hockey at the school and on the pond by the Armstrong barn, which was just across the road. There were lots of hills near the school where we went tobogganing, and we skied all over the hills. I remember one time we went to get a Christmas tree for the school. The ceiling in the school was maybe 10 feet high. We brought a 30-foot tree back to the school and we pushed it and struggled with it, but we got it up there!"

Jarvis graduated from the one-room schoolhouse just in time. Only a few years later, in 1961, all four schoolhouses in the township — the others being Highland, built in 1902; McCool, built in 1904; and Kerns and Armstrong, built in 1905 — were closed and the students amalgamated into the newly erected Kerns Central Public School. The decision drove another nail into Milberta's coffin. There would be no opportunity for rebirth.

When Milberta's school shut down, the only remaining community amenity was the United Church — the Methodist congregation of the

Highland Settlement had joined with its Presbyterian brethren in 1917. There was a time when people feared losing this landmark, as well. Although rebuilt in the early 1940s, by the 1990s, the aging church was in dire need of further renovation. The building was aging poorly and was desperately out of date, with no washrooms and insufficient heating. Would the community rally to find the funds, or would the church hold a solemn farewell service and close?

Thankfully, the community came together, just as it had in 1903, when its citizens built the church in the first place, and raised the necessary funds. Extensive restoration and modernization followed. An addition was built to provide a better entrance and indoor washroom facilities. The interior was completely insulated and drywalled, while the exterior was clad in vinyl siding. So while the Presbyterian church looks far different, it nonetheless remains a beacon of hope in the one-time village to this day, even as it celebrates 120 years. Sadly, its future is currently up in the air, and there is the possibility that the church might be dismantled.

An 80-year-old road grader sits beside Milberta's church. When the village was founded, there was no road. Settlers and goods were transported by boat along the Wabi River from Lake Temiskaming.

Those who resided in Milberta in the early 20th century wouldn't recognize the place today. The main street lined with sidewalks and businesses? Gone. It's just a road today. The mills, the school, the stores — they're all gone, too. And yet, unlike many ghost communities across Ontario's cottage country, farming continues here. The fields are green and lush under clear blue skies, evidence that early settlers didn't misplace their faith this region could be bountiful.

As the shapes of small rural communities change and many slowly fade away, nostalgia proliferates online in wistful memorializing of "the good old days." This reminiscing is a chance to discover not only our past but also to discover what these villages and towns — ghost towns in particular — have to teach us about the real human need for a sense of community.

In a region of dense forest and harsh climate, described as seven months of snow, two of summer, and plenty of blackflies and mosquitoes, Milberta could only have been settled and then developed by people sharing a joint purpose — a true community.

 To Get There

Follow Highway 65 northwest from New Liskeard. Milberta Road is on the north. Kerns, or Milberta Cemetery, where so many of the early settlers were buried, is located at the end of Highland Road, which runs off Milberta Road. For the site of the village proper, continue north on Milberta Road until it meets North Quarry Road, Concession 3. When you see the Milberta United Church, you've arrived. The sidewalk fronting the string of businesses was on the opposite side of the road, running from the church north to the intersection. No exploration of Milberta's history is complete without a visit to the Little Claybelt Homesteaders Museum in New Liskeard (claybeltmuseum.ca), located just east of the intersection of Highways 11 and 65. A fine museum with immersive exhibits, you'll leave with a better appreciation of the region's past.

ACKNOWLEDGEMENTS

To complete this book, I was, as is always the case with such projects, dependent on the help of a lot of people. The list of people to whom I'm indebted is far too long to name here but suffice to say I thank you all.

I'd also like to extend a warm thank you to the many museums and libraries that have proven invaluable on many occasions.

To my parents, thank you for all your support over the years. And to my long-suffering family, thank you — to Claire, for inspiring me to both be a better writer and a better person, and to Nicoletta, for always being there for me. I don't know what I'd do without you.

SOURCES

Archives and Museums

Algonquin Loggers Museum (algonquinpark.on.ca/visit/locations/algonquin
-logging-museum.php).

Algonquin Park Archives (algonquinpark.on.ca/visit/history/algonquin-park
-archives.php).

Burk's Falls Museums (burksfalls.net/my-community/museums).

Haliburton Highlands Museum (haliburtonhighlandsmuseum.com).

Humphrey Museum (seguin.ca/en/explore-play/humphreymuseum.aspx).

Little Claybelt Homesteaders Museum (claybeltmuseum.ca).

Magnetawan Historical Museum (magnetawan.com/explore/places-to-visit
/museums/heritage-centre).

Minden Hills Museum and Heritage Village (mindenhills.ca/en/things-to-do
/museum-and-heritage-village.aspx).

Stanhope Heritage Discovery Museum (stanhopemuseum.on.ca).

Sturgeon River House Museum (westnipissing.ca/culture-recreation/sturgeon
  -river-house-museum).
West Parry Sound District Museum on Tower Hill (museumontowerhill.com).

Books

Boyer, Robert J. *A Good Town Grew Here: The Story of Bracebridge*. Bracebridge,
  ON: Oxbow Press, 1975.
Christie Historical Society. *Meanderings and Memories*. Christie Township, ON:
  Christie Historical Society, 1994.
Coombe, Geraldine. *Muskoka Past and Present*. Toronto: McGraw-Ryerson, 1976.
Cotton, Larry D. *Whiskey and Wickedness, Volume 3: Muskoka and Parry Sound
  Districts*. Barrie, ON: Larry Cotton and Associates, 2004.
Da Silva, Maria, and Andrew Hind. *Ghost Towns of Muskoka*. Toronto: Dundurn,
  2008.
Denniss, Gary. *A Brief History of the Churches of Muskoka*. Bracebridge, ON:
  Self-published, 2002.
____. *A Brief History of the Schools in Muskoka*. Bracebridge, ON: Herald-Gazette
  Press, 1972.
____. *The Spirit of the Twelfth*. Bracebridge, ON: Self-published, 1982.
Haliburton Highlands History Committee. *Haliburton: A History in Pictures*.
  Self-published, 2008.
Hall, R.W. *History of Royston*. Self-published.
Hamilton, W.E., ed. *Guide Book and Atlas of Muskoka and Parry Sound Districts*.
  Toronto: H.R. Page, 1879.
Hind, Andrew. *Founded on Stone: Tales of Early Parry Sound District*. Self-
  published, 2020.
____. *Founded on Stone 2: More Tales of Early Parry Sound District*. Self-published,
  2022.
Macfie, John. *Lots More ... Parry Sound Stories*. Parry Sound, ON: The Hay
  Press, 2005.
____. *Parry Sound Logging Days*. Toronto: Boston Mills Press, 1987.
____. *Still More ... Parry Sound Stories*. Self-published, 2014.

_____. *Tales from Another Time*. Parry Sound, ON: The Hay Press, 2000.

Mackey, Doug. *Kiosk. The Saga of Life, Logging and Lumbering in and Around Northwest Algonquin Park*. Toronto: Past Forward Heritage, 2007.

Madill, Janice. *A Track Through Time: A History of the Township of McMurrich*. Self-published, 1994.

Milberta Community Women. *Kerns Township*. New Liskeard, ON: Little Claybelt Homesteaders Museum.

Mulvany, Charles Pelham. *History of the County of Peterborough, Ontario*. Toronto: C. Blackett Robinson, 1884.

Ryerson Book Committee. *A Tribute to Ryerson Township 1880–1980*. Sprucedale, ON: Olympic Publishing, 1980.

Stewart, Helen. *In Celebration of the Old Nipissing Road 1875–2000*. Magnetawan, ON: Arrow Printing and Publishing, 2000.

Tatley, Richard. *The Steamboat Era in the Muskokas, Vol. I: To the Golden Years*. Toronto: Boston Mills Press, 1983.

_____. *The Steamboat Era in the Muskokas, Vol. II: The Golden Years to the Present*. Toronto: Boston Mills Press, 1983.

Taylor, Bruce W. *Place Names of Temiskaming*. Cobalt, ON: White Mountain Publications, 2006.

Interviews

Allen, William

Brown, Merv

Brown, Ron

Burk, Paul

Clark, Godfrey

Evans, Patricia Moore

Fitzmaurice, Mary

Gilbert, Velda

Haslehurst, Donna

Herring, Vera

MacDonald, Gayle

McKinnon, Shane
Mour, Jen
Pahkala, Elizabeth Beatty
Patterson, Deborah
Rance, Lisa
Sword, Arline
Sword, Jack
Thomas, Viola (née Bell)
Triemstra, Nadine
Truax, Bev
Valade, Amber

Newspapers

Bracebridge Herald-Gazette
Burk's Falls Arrow
Daily British Whig
Haliburton Times
Muskoka Herald
Muskoka Sun
Newmarket Era
Toronto Daily Star

Unpublished Manuscripts

"Guestbook SS No. 2 Ryerson Township."
"Milberta Tweedsmuir History Book."
"Reminiscences of Dan Jarvis, 2020" (provided by Little Claybelt Homesteaders Museum).
"Reminiscences of Iva Irwin" (provided by Ron Brown).
"Reminiscences of Minnie May River, 1977" (provided by Carol Moffat).
"Temiskaming Women's Institute Book."

IMAGE CREDITS

INDEX

ABOUT THE AUTHOR

Andrew Hind was born in North York, Ontario, and has been interested in history for as long as he can remember. As a freelance writer, he specializes in history, travel, and lifestyle, and has a deep passion for Ontario's cottage country. Over the course of a 20-year writing career, he has contributed to count-less publications, among them *Parry Sound Life*, *Muskoka Life*, *Canada's History*, and many more.

Ghost Towns of Ontario's Cottage Country is Andrew's thirtieth book, the fifth for Dundurn. Previous Dundurn titles include *Ghost Towns of Muskoka*, *RMS Segwun: Queen of Muskoka*, *Muskoka Resorts: Then and Now*, and *Ghosts of Niagara-on-the-Lake*.

Andrew is the proudest of fathers to a five-year-old daughter who loves writing on Daddy's computer. Her royalties are paid in Smarties.